SHOE
strology

SHOE
strology

DISCOVER YOUR BIRTHDAY SHOE

★

The AstroTwins, Tali & Ophira Edut
Illustrations by Samantha Hahn

Potter Style ★ New York

Potter Style

ISBN 978-0-307-98504-0
eISBN 978-0770-43330-7

Printed in China

10 9 8 7 6 5 4 3 2 1

First Edition

Text by Tali and Ophira Edut ★ ***Illustrations by*** Samantha Hahn ★ ***Design by*** Danielle Deschenes

Introduction

Shoes have as much personality as the stylish women who select them. Based on the day you were born, *Shoestrology* is a soul-to-sole guide to understanding your unique traits. A shoe has been carefully selected and hand-illustrated for each day of the year, combining the ancient art of astrology and the bespoke magic of fashion.

From the classic Chanel ballet slipper to the dazzling Louboutin pump, there's a shoe that fits every woman. Which shoe best describes you? Flip to your birthday page to find out! The shoe chosen for your birthday may be one that you'd proudly wear; or, it may merely be a metaphor of your basic makeup. This book can also serve as a guide to understanding the people in your life, and perhaps finding your "sole-mate" among the pages.

What girl doesn't dream about stepping into beautiful pumps, stilettos, sandals, and boots? From vintage Dior to the magic of McQueen, with 366 gorgeous pairs to admire, *Shoestrology* is like walking through your own incredible collection of shoes.

Capricorn December 22–January 20

JAN·UARY

January 21–February 19 Aquarius

January 1

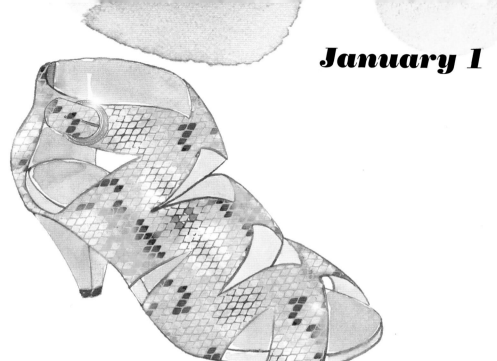

As the reigning queen of practical magic, you know that form must follow function. A well-structured sandal with a low heel and an ankle strap elevate you to a perfectly dignified level. The unique cutaways show your keen sense of balance and modesty. You always reveal just enough of yourself to keep people intrigued, but never so much that you're an open book. Building things of lasting value is one of your strengths, and you show your sparkle through muted metallic snakeskin fabric. A glimmer of glamour is all you need to captivate the world's attention.

Kick It Up WARM, ELEGANT, PRACTICAL   *Step It Down* ELITIST, SECRETIVE

January 2

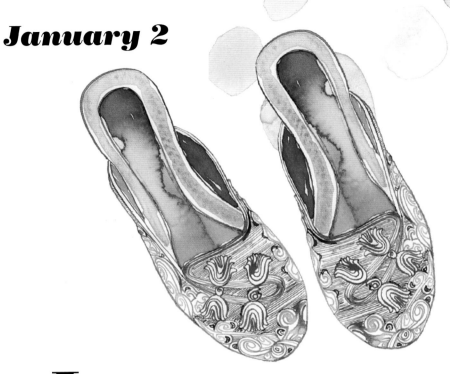

Like the original owner of these nineteenth-century Turkish slippers, you are an individual who naturally rises to a place of status. You have a quiet, intuitive wisdom that leaves people feeling nurtured and safe in your presence. During the days of the Ottoman Empire, these delicately crafted slippers were donned only when a woman was welcoming honored guests to her home. As an innately captivating hostess, you will have prestigious and fascinating people circled around your hearth throughout your life. The fine embroidery mirrors your attention to quality and detail. If anyone knows how to appreciate the little things—especially the gorgeous ones—it is surely you.

Kick It Up NURTURING, INTUITIVE, CARING   *Step It Down* FUSSY, INVISIBLE

You are a pillar of society, and like this stunning Gucci "Malika" platform sandal, you naturally elevate yourself to breathtaking heights. Your jovial, larger-than-life personality is well suited to the green piped velvet and bold stiletto on this shoe, and you don't mind making a spectacle of yourself from time to time. You have a bountiful vision, which keeps you a few steps ahead of the game as a leader. Always au courant, you are a trendsetter who is also a touch of a traditionalist. As such, you like to walk among the best of the best when you are setting up the team for one of your many trailblazing missions.

January 3

Kick It Up ENTERPRISING, CHARMING, HUMOROUS *Step It Down* SUPERIOR, COMPETITIVE

January 4

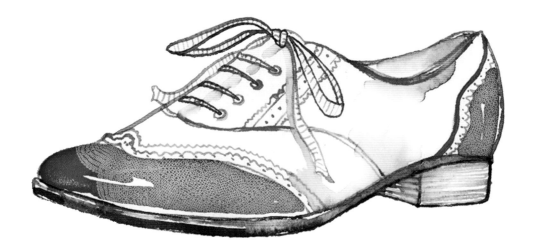

Like this menswear-inspired, wingtip oxford, you can hold your own around both the ladies and the fellas. Old Boys' Club, be damned! With your tremendous ambition and unmatchable drive, you naturally find your place among the highest ranks. There's nothing forceful about your ascent to success. You'll earn your rightful place among the power players on the strength of your merit and hard work, even if it takes years to make the climb. When you inevitably reach the top, you love to teach others how to do the same. Like this classic shoe, you always have your feet planted firmly on the ground, but you definitely have plenty of panache to share with the world!

Kick It Up AUTHORITATIVE, SKILLFUL, MODEST   *Step It Down* PESSIMISTIC, STUBBORN

January 5

The 1950s was an era of traditional values, and while you're hardly the subservient type, you find beauty in the "good old days," when family came first and life was, well, simpler. Like these June Cleaver–esque pumps, you are classic to the core. If you're going to bake a cake, lunch with the ladies, or head up a PTA initiative, you might as well look good doing it. You have a curious mind that makes you eager to absorb new information. You'll weigh this knowledge carefully against conventional wisdom, artfully synthesizing the old with the new. This is what makes you thoroughly modern and timeless at once, much like these shoes that never goes out of style.

Kick It Up CURIOUS, LOYAL, STRAIGHTFORWARD   *Step It Down* STUBBORN, CUTTHROAT

January 6

Sign ★ CAPRICORN

Your keen foresight and knowing feelings regularly save people from dangerous missteps, much like the revered French warrior Joan of Arc. You are a saint in the eyes of those who know you—a status well earned by your devotion, loyalty, and willingness to put it all on the line when you feel something is worth fighting for. These boots, a replica of the ones Joan of Arc wore as a "white knight," were polished to such a gleam that she was said to glow like an ethereal being as she set forth to do battle. When you are on a mission, you radiate in much the same way, especially when you are able to bring your profound emotions and creativity into your arsenal.

Kick It Up PASSIONATE, DEVOTED, INTUITIVE   *Step It Down* CODEPENDENT, RECKLESS

January 7

You are a highly determined individual who is willing to go the distance to get what she wants. You are dreamy and imaginative without losing touch with the earth beneath your feet. These colorful Indian slippers, the likes of which are worn by Bollywood actresses, help you to glide and dance through life, dazzling people with your charm and dexterity. Like the golden floss intertwined in these slippers, you can take a thread of an idea and weave it into a magical and memorable experience for those around you. Perhaps it's all an illusion, but that's not the point: You are highlighting new possibilities for people and elegantly lifting them into new realms of thought.

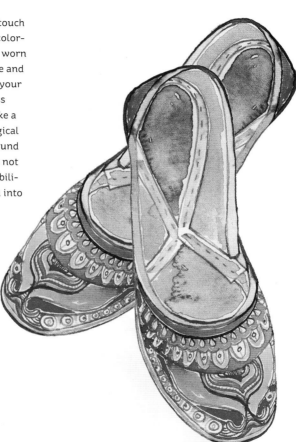

Sign ★ CAPRICORN

Kick It Up IMAGINATIVE, AGILE, DAZZLING   ***Step It Down*** PREOCCUPIED, FLIGHTY

January 8

Like the classic moccasin, you are earthy and resilient, capable of standing up to the toughest conditions. Where most people would veer from challenges, you invite them into your life, knowing that you'll grow ever stronger with each test of wills that you pass. Among their Native American originators, moccasins were so carefully crafted with subtle variations in stitching and heel shape that tribes could distinguish one another from the footprint the shoe left behind. Indeed, you are an expert tracker. When you want something, you'll hunt it down with unflagging resolve, finding just the right people to connect you to the resources you need.

Kick It Up DURABLE, AMBITIOUS, UNIQUE   *Step It Down* HARDENED, BRUSQUE

January 9

Round 'em up and rope 'em in: few can resist the circle of your magic lasso. You're a born leader who believes in remaining staunchly down to earth in spite of your considerable influence. Your rodeo queen sisters share your spirit. The classic cowgirls were nearly indistinguishable from the cowboys, with one exception—like this hand-tooled boot, they preferred a bit more color and flash. That's how you navigate through life, breaking down traditional gender roles without overturning the valuable systems that are already in place. Your primary goals are to master your craft and earn genuine respect. If you're going to make a spectacle of yourself, it's going to be done with a skill that kicks some ass!

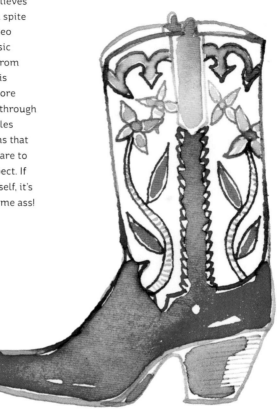

Sign ★ CAPRICORN

Kick It Up HUMBLE, HARDWORKING, SKILLED   *Step It Down* TUNNEL-VISIONED, AUSTERE

January 10

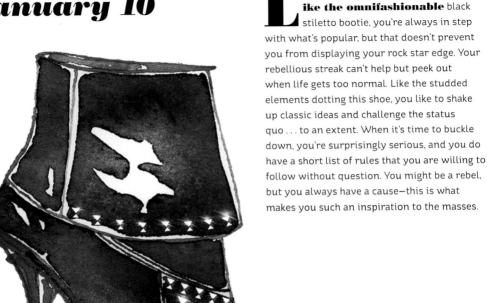

Like the omnifashionable black stiletto bootie, you're always in step with what's popular, but that doesn't prevent you from displaying your rock star edge. Your rebellious streak can't help but peek out when life gets too normal. Like the studded elements dotting this shoe, you like to shake up classic ideas and challenge the status quo . . . to an extent. When it's time to buckle down, you're surprisingly serious, and you do have a short list of rules that you are willing to follow without question. You might be a rebel, but you always have a cause—this is what makes you such an inspiration to the masses.

Kick It Up ORIGINAL, DARING, DEDICATED   *Step It Down* DESTRUCTIVE, ARGUMENTATIVE

January 11

Like this animal print stiletto, you know that being fierce doesn't have to mean "in your face." You're capable of projecting a neutral energy, even when you are fighting for a higher cause. That gracious gift allows you to win formidable allies and to "change the system from within." Like a leopard's intricate spots, you may have some habitual patterns, but you are not predictable by any stretch of the imagination. People are often left guessing what you'll do next. Small surprises are your favorite form of shock value since you innately understand that subtle shifts can create big ripples of change.

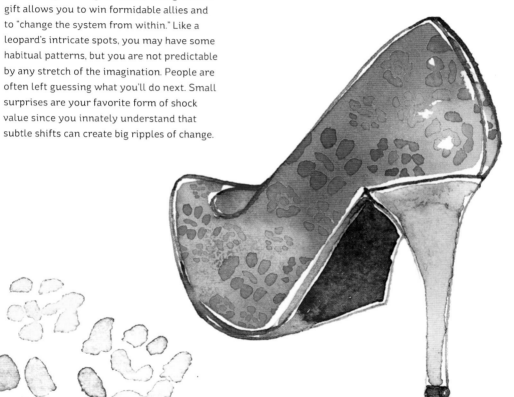

Sign ★ CAPRICORN

Kick It Up CALM, HIGH-MINDED, FAIR   ***Step It Down*** HAUGHTY, COLD

January 12

This 1940s peep-toe slingback was born in an era of transition. Wartime was ending, but resources were still scant. There is a practical magic to this shoe, which, like you, manages to be sensibly sexy. The low wedge heel helps you remain in balance as you dance to the beat of your own drummer, and the open toe was considered flirty without being vulgar. Like the 1940s, transitions seem to be a grand theme in your own life. You gravitate toward situations that have a temporary quality to them, taking each one on as an insightful learning opportunity. Brilliantly and generously, you allow other people to see you sweat through the process. Ultimately you'll triumph, and your struggles will become a source of inspiration for the public.

Kick It Up ENTHUSIASTIC, CAPRICIOUS, FUN-LOVING   **Step It Down** INDULGENT, RISKY

January 13

Laughter is the best medicine, and with your wry, intelligent wit, you administer large doses of humor like a resident MD. Just as the comedy and tragedy masks hang side by side in theatrical symbolism, you may be a wisecracker, but you also understand the soulful depths of suffering. The twin themes of joy and despair are ones you can navigate fluidly, giving you a deep sense of compassion for humankind. There's a measure of truth behind every joke, and your candor is so relatable that it helps lift people out of the doldrums. The slightly curled toe of this seventeenth-century-style shoe conjures up images of the medieval jester, who was never thought to be a clown, but rather a privileged member of the royal court whose jokes were divinely inspired.

Kick It Up HILARIOUS, OUTSPOKEN, COMPASSIONATE   *Step It Down* HARSH, SELF-DEPRECATING

January 14

No peeking! Like this Victorian bootie, you believe in retaining an air of mystery and modesty. This sturdy shoe was born in a time when the ankle and leg were considered "naughty bits." Catching even a glimpse of a lady's leg was downright erotic! In much the same way, you know that covering up certain aspects of yourself only makes you all the more alluring. What's going on beneath the surface of your mystique? You'd rather leave them wondering until they've earned the right to peek beneath your floor-grazing hemline. It's not that you're conservative; you're just 100 percent certain that the best things come to those who are willing to wait. Patience and perseverance are your strong suits as you keep it all in stride.

Kick It Up TENACIOUS, MEASURED, CALM   ***Step It Down*** UNADVENTUROUS, PRUDISH

January 15

Vivacious and flamboyant, you have a risqué edge that cannot be repressed. The whimsically adorned shoes worn by 1920s flappers symbolize your loud and proud persona. Sexuality and femininity, you believe, should be touted with pride, not shame: If you've got it, flaunt it . . . and own it! Your bejeweled heels sparkle with stunning brilliance, yet they are low enough to allow you to dance through life without tripping yourself up. The cleverly engineered T-strap gives you stylish support as you blaze the trails of liberation. Early in life, you may be the studious "good girl," but once you've found your mission, you'll gloriously and publicly demonstrate the very change you wish to see in the world.

Sign ★ CAPRICORN

Kick It Up VALIANCE, SPARKLE, ATTITUDE ***Step It Down*** BAWDINESS, BAD TIMING

January 16

Sign ★ CAPRICORN

Dreamy and levelheaded at once, you're a contradiction unto yourself. There's an ethereal quality to you, as if you might defy the laws of gravity and lift yourself into flight. Then there's your earthy sensuality that makes it clear you have your feet firmly planted on the ground. Like these handmade leather African gladiator sandals, you like to wrap your life up with a minimal measure of structure. The delicately beaded ankle strap helps you remain earthbound until you hitch your wagon to the next star. Your life is ever evolving; you're not afraid to topple the old structures when it's time to rebuild from the ground up.

Kick It Up SENSUAL, DREAMY, GODDESSLIKE *Step It Down* ABSENTMINDED, REMOTE

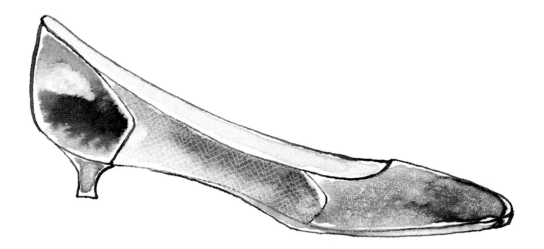

Like the brushed metallic leather of this kitten-heeled pump, you shimmer in an elegant, gracious, and classic way. Your values tend toward the modest side of the spectrum, and you hate to make a spectacle of yourself. That said, you are willing to step into a prominent public position if it means making a difference for a cause. Eloquent to the core, you are the ideal spokeswoman, inspiring people with uncomplicated solutions that are easy to implement. Like the low heel of this shoe, you prefer to remain toe-to-toe and eye-to-eye with the everyday person, growing organically through common wisdom, good health, and practiced restraint.

Kick It Up POLISHED, RELATABLE, DEDICATED   *Step It Down* OFFICIOUS, UPTIGHT

January 18

Sign ★ CAPRICORN

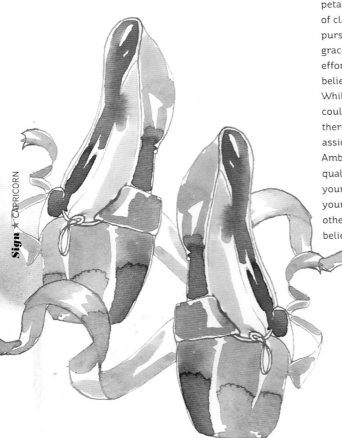

Fantasy? Reality? You prefer to keep a foot in both worlds. Like the petal-pink ballet slipper, you are a symbol of classic elegance and hard-won creative pursuits. As if you're floating on air, your graceful and playful nature appears to arise effortlessly from your soul; however, this belies the truth about your tireless work ethic. While your pursuits may be fanciful, they could hardly be labeled flights of fancy. If there's a dream to be manifested, you'll train assiduously until the desired goal is achieved. Ambition, and at times perfectionism, is a quality that's woven into the very fiber of your being. Once you feel "on pointe" with your skills, you're a vision to behold, inspiring others to lift themselves higher than they believe they're capable of.

Kick It Up IMAGINATIVE, INSPIRED, DEDICATED   **Step It Down** OVERWORKED, SELF-CRITICAL

With your can-do spirit, you are ready to kick up your heels at a moment's notice, approaching each chapter of life with sunshine-bright optimism. You have a taste for luxury and enjoy the finer things. And why shouldn't you? You work hard for your money, and it's well within your rights to enjoy a little flash and glitz. Celebrations are your favorite thing, especially if they go along with traditions that are near and dear to your heart. Like this golden stiletto mule, you love situations that lift you to an exhilarating high. When it's time to kick off your shoes and get down and dirty, you're equally game, and you don't want any fussy straps and buckles standing in your way.

Sign ★ CAPRICORN

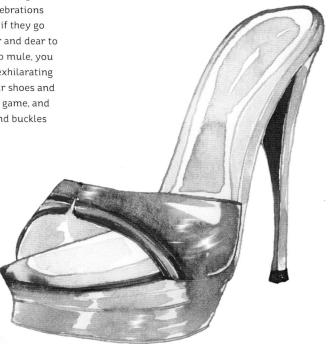

Kick It Up ELECTRIC, CREATIVE, INFLUENTIAL   *Step It Down* UNSTABLE, SELF-DESTRUCTIVE

January 20

Sign ★ CAPRICORN

An intrepid voyager, you journey through life with an innate sense of curiosity. Just like the mukluk, you'll weather harsh conditions and traverse barren landscapes in search of an exalted goal. There's no stopping you when you've got your eyes fixed on a prize, particularly one with a humanitarian bent. You are an adventurer whose compass spins in many directions. Your friendly, genuine nature wins you friends in every port—many of whom you'll keep throughout the years. Like the pompoms adorning this winter boot, you've got flair and character that set you apart from the masses. Some would call you offbeat, even eccentric. You won't argue there. Being original is a badge of pride, as far as you're concerned.

Kick It Up INQUISITIVE, ADVENTUROUS, BOLD   *Step It Down* DETACHED, ALOOF

January 21

Your gypsy soul was born to roam, leaving a mystical trail of stardust with each footprint. Although you're worldly, you don't quite feel "of this world." There is a part of you that prefers to remain on the outside, observing people through a keen and poetic lens. Like this elaborate Chanel boot, your life is a rich, complex tapestry of disparate elements. You twinkle without being gaudy, sparkle without being gauche, weaving together influences from many cultures and eras. Your migration path is fascinating and unpredictable—it's anyone's guess where you'll take your next step.

Kick It Up ENCHANTING, POETIC, ENIGMATIC *Step It Down* ELUSIVE, ANTISOCIAL

January 22

Sign ★ AQUARIUS

Like this outrageous knee-high go-go boot, you're futuristic, wild, and a total free spirit. You love being the first one to step out with a new idea, even if it has yet to be fully proved. That's because you're also a bit of a mad scientist, willing to experiment, fail, and blow up the chemistry lab until you discover your "Eureka!" moment. Community-oriented, you easily find yourself at the epicenter of avant-garde movements, collecting friends every step of the way. The one thing you hate? When people try to limit your freedom and self-expression. That's when you rocket off to a new galaxy, leaving them eating your stardust.

Kick It Up WILD, FREEDOM-LOVING, INVENTIVE ***Step It Down*** EXPLOSIVE, RECKLESS

Like these sporty, slip-on sneakers, you're accessible, friendly, and comfortable to be around. Even when you're showing your more offbeat stripes, you remain in step with what's the latest. Thus people look to you as a trendsetter—a role you naturally step in to. Your popularity arises from your fresh-faced, girl-next-door charm, but surprise, surprise: you've also got plenty of edge. There's a sass about you, which allows you to playfully disagree with people and to debate without being argumentative. Your mind is sharp and inquisitive. Discussing and exploring new ideas is one of your favorite things, and you're often the first girl on the block to rock a stylin' haircut or carry a hip new gadget in her purse.

Kick It Up FRIENDLY, ACCEPTING, WITTY   ***Step It Down*** GLIB, WASTEFUL

January 24

Creative and relationship-oriented, you don't break down doors by sheer force. You do so by making genuine connections with people, so that they graciously invite you to glide on over their thresholds. Like these 1930s marabou slippers, you carry yourself with an elegantly passionate flair, but you also have a comfortable presence about you. A deep thinker and a lover, your rational mind and heart are often at odds with each other. When they do sync up, you are highly intuitive, helping you connect to people in a profound and memorable way. You may lead a rich life of legendary romantic encounters, but having work that you love is as essential to your happiness as finding the right mate.

Kick It Up ADMIRED, ACTIVE, MAGNETIC   *Step It Down* SELF-CENTERED, ELITIST

January 25

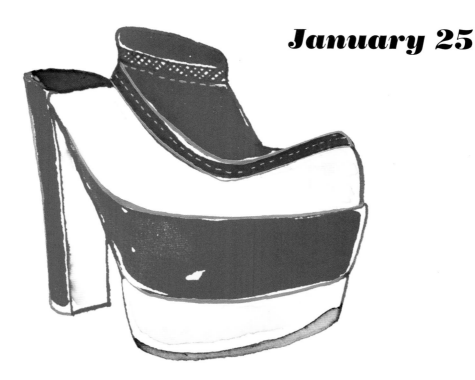

Sign ★ AQUARIUS

Like this groovy 1970s platform clog, you take an elevated view of the world, peering through the eyes of a rebel and a revolutionary. Without a doubt, you're here to shake up the status quo, surprising and delighting people with your enchanting vision. The sky is hardly the limit for your ever-expanding horizons. You want to journey to outer space and plunge to the deepest realms of your consciousness. Sometimes, the hardest place for you to be is Planet Earth. Your tribemates are few and far between, making you feel a bit like an alien sometimes. When you muster up the courage to articulate your unique vision, you find yourself soaring up the popularity charts, collecting friends from all walks of life.

Kick It Up SOULFUL, INVENTIVE, REVOLUTIONARY   *Step It Down* SPACEY, ISOLATED

January 26

Sign ★ AQUARIUS

You live by your convictions and are ruled by your ideals—and no one can move you once you've taken a strong stance. This lace-up combat boot signifies your fighting spirit, which often emerges when it's time to defend the underdog. Equality, you believe, is everyone's birthright. You're both a capable foot soldier and a tactical general when it's time to rally for a cause. Self-disciplined, you are willing to go without flashy bells and whistles if it means creating enough resources to share with everyone. Like this toughened leather, you may have a hard shell to pierce. Nonetheless, you are a team player who loves her friends with a passion. You always find creative ways to express your individual facets, much like the small metal embellishments dotting the surface of these boots.

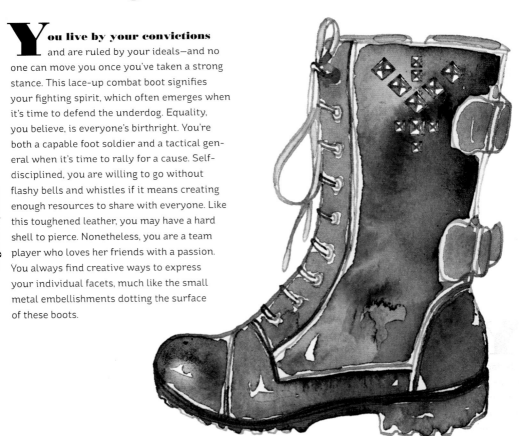

Kick It Up FIERCE, STEADFAST, TEAM-SPIRITED   *Step It Down* EXTREME, RECKLESS

You are charmingly strong willed, a woman who knows what she wants and won't stop until she gets it. Like this 1940s babydoll heel, you can be perfectly ladylike when interfacing with the public. It's behind the scenes where you work your greatest magic. The mesh weave and spat-inspired detailing that make up this pump show the clever use of materials during the wartime era, when leather was scant. Similarly, you are quite the resourceful one, skilled at the art of "making something out of nothing" and impressing people with your capable creativity. You can be impulsive at times, and a wee bit secretive, especially when you fear people will judge you for your more eccentric—and even radical—ideas.

Kick It Up RESOURCEFUL, INNOVATIVE, ORIGINAL   *Step It Down* ANXIOUS, SECRETIVE

January 28

Like this tinkling chain-strap sandal, you are not only charm personified, but you also serve as a lucky charm for the ones who love you. Where their belief flags, you step in with the power of an entire fleet of motivational coaches, coaxing them to see the bright side in a loving, playful way. This magical quality makes you the best friend to have around. You believe in the power of the human spirit, gathering people together for a meaningful moment whenever you can. No one would ever accuse you of being flighty, though. There's a technical competence that comes along with your keen ideas, and you radiate an aura of "geek chic."

Kick It Up WHIMSICAL, ENDEARING, MAGICAL ***Step It Down*** ERRATIC, UNFOCUSED

You are the ultimate team player, a born people person who always thinks about the "we" before the "me." Collaborating around a vision is one of your greatest joys in life. While you're a natural leader, you play more of a facilitator's role, creating the backdrop that allows others to shine along with you. These classic Converse All-Star sneakers were once worn exclusively by professional b-ballers. Now, they are embraced by athletes and the stylish set alike. You too have that universal appeal, and an ability to connect with people from all walks of life and find the common thread that laces you all together. The desire to master a craft will be strong throughout your life, which you will accomplish in a modest, organic, and inspiring way.

Kick It Up POPULAR, GENEROUS, BROAD-MINDED   *Step It Down* RESTRAINED, PEOPLE-PLEASING

January 30

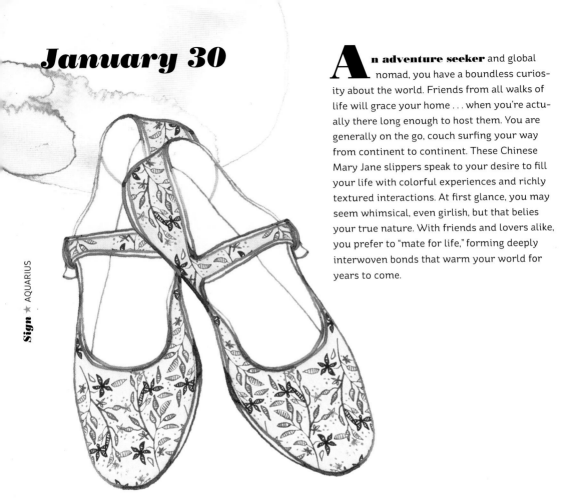

An adventure seeker and global nomad, you have a boundless curiosity about the world. Friends from all walks of life will grace your home . . . when you're actually there long enough to host them. You are generally on the go, couch surfing your way from continent to continent. These Chinese Mary Jane slippers speak to your desire to fill your life with colorful experiences and richly textured interactions. At first glance, you may seem whimsical, even girlish, but that belies your true nature. With friends and lovers alike, you prefer to "mate for life," forming deeply interwoven bonds that warm your world for years to come.

Kick It Up FANCIFUL, MULTIFACETED, WORLDLY   ***Step It Down*** UNREACHABLE, FLIGHTY

January 31

Like these vintage motorcycle boots, you have a weighty presence. People sit up and take notice when you clomp into a room. Paradoxically, you aren't exactly gunning for a position of power in this lifetime. Being "down with the people" is your preference, especially since your own relationship with authority figures can be testy. Like these boots, which have come to symbolize the kick-ass rebel, you like to stir the pot. Anger is a touchstone emotion for you: when something fires you up, you want to jump up and do something about it. You enjoy being around people who are both quirky and down to earth, and while your own appearance is stylishly unpolished, you never have a problem helping other people shine.

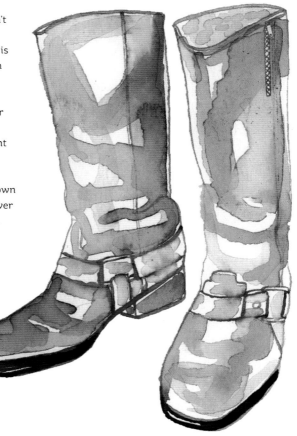

Kick It Up UNPRETENTIOUS, SUPPORTIVE, FUN **Step It Down** HOTHEADED, CONTRARIAN

January 21–February 19 *Aquarius*

FEB· RU· ARY

February 20–March 19 *Pisces*

February 1

You're a multifaceted talent who likes to have her hands in many pots. Like these cute and quirky peep-toe Mary Janes from Seychelles, your offbeat edge is at the heart of your charm. People watch to see what you'll do next, as you seem to have your finger directly on the zeitgeist's pulse. Like the shoe's neutral gray hue, you're never so over the top as to alienate people. Quite the contrary: without any effort to fit in, you naturally become popular, a stylish trendsetter whose ideas are bound to catch on like wildfire.

Kick It Up ACTIVE, POPULAR, TRENDSETTING   *Step It Down* SCATTERED, IMPULSIVE

February 2

With their rhythmic *clack, clack, clack,* these early-twentieth-century Japanese geta are usually heard before they are seen. As one who stirs up intrigue wherever she goes, your legend also precedes you. Skill and grace are required to successfully maneuver these shoes, which were worn historically by geisha to elevate their kimonos from the ground. Polished, sophisticated, and sexy, you are able to make complicated tasks appear easy. Behind the scenes, however, you'll work tirelessly to master your craft until you are ready to make your elegant debut.

Kick It Up INTRIGUING, POLISHED, HARDWORKING   ***Step It Down*** ENIGMATIC, OBSESSIVE

February 3

You're an intellectual bohemian who is fascinated with new ideas, avant-garde social movements, and anything that piques the curiosity of your whip-smart brain. This Alexander Wang "Trish" loafer mule is all business in the front, and indeed you can come across as serious and professional when needed. The capricious wedge says, "You don't own me," a tip to your liberated outlook on life. It's a shoe that could easily be seen dangling from the foot of an intrepid journalist, social activist, or other trendsetter who shares your passion for sticking up for the underdog. Your life path involves changing the world for the everyday citizen. Power to the people!

Kick It Up AVANT-GARDE, INTELLECTUAL, AWARE   ***Step It Down*** REBELLIOUS, ARGUMENTATIVE

February 4

The crystal-encrusted exterior of this Alexander McQueen boot echoes nature's own miraculous formations. There is an innate wisdom to the crystals' repetitive shape and glow, something that clearly took genius to cultivate. A virtuoso in your own right, you understand this best, shining through your tenacity, especially when you are devoted to a cause. You aren't afraid to divert from the norm, making a statement as spellbinding as this boot's faceted heel. An initiator, you might spark a movement with one simple act, like civil rights heroine Rosa Parks, who shares your birthday.

Kick It Up TENACIOUS, GENIUS, COURAGEOUS   *Step It Down* SELF-DEPRECATING, PRICKLY

If there's a needle in a haystack, you'll be the one to unearth it. This famously hard-to-find Manolo Blahnik Mary Jane was featured in an episode of *Sex and the City*. Hiding in the *Vogue* magazine fashion closet, it was discovered by a delighted Carrie Bradshaw. You treasure the rare and unusual, and you'll travel to the ends of the universe to collect, study, and experience such singular delights. Like this sophisticated heel, you project a cool, collected, and confident aura. You are also an object of desire in your own right, your company coveted by many.

Kick It Up DESIRABLE, PASSIONATE, SOPHISTICATED   *Step It Down* INTIMIDATING, FANATICAL

February 6

This custom-dyed Converse high-top is a throwback to the Summer of Love. If you could transport yourself back to 1967, you'd surely find yourself in San Francisco, wandering down Haight Street, wearing flowers in your hair. Naturally popular, you make friends wherever you go. For you, it's not about fitting in, but rather about standing out. Your colorful personality is as bright and appealing as the psychedelic wash on these trainers. As a friend, you're as supportive as they come. You're always there to cheer on your pals, encouraging them to express themselves boldly and develop their own nonconformist styles.

Kick It Up SOCIAL, COLORFUL, SUPPORTIVE   *Step It Down* ADRIFT, OVERLY TRUSTING

With its oversize bow and cheery upturned toe, this Irregular Choice heel has a fresh, childlike appeal. As someone who never loses touch with the kid inside of her, you love anything that alludes to the days of unfiltered innocence. You may spend your life creating a world that is safe and encouraging for children, or inviting "kids of all ages" to continue to play long after their graduation caps have been tossed in the air. Peter Pan, whose suit rivals the playfulness of these shoes, promised to never grow up. You're right there with him, delighting people with your irrepressibly entertaining ideas.

Kick It Up PLAYFUL, IMAGINATIVE, UPLIFTING   *Step It Down* OVERINDULGENT, BRATTY

February 8

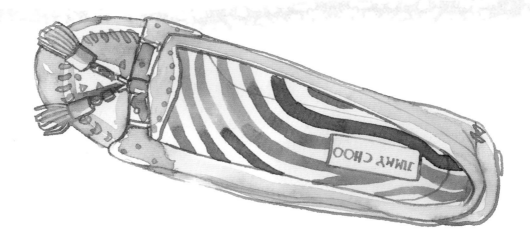

You walk with the calm of a tribal elder, gracefully navigating dynamics that would trip most people up. People see you as a leader, the wise soul they can lean on. "Zephyr," Jimmy Choo's modernized spin on the classic moccasin, helps you stay anchored in your role of the chief. The studs and tassels lend a fun feel; perfect for someone who knows that laughter is the soul's best medicine. The snappy zebra-print lining is an added bonus, a nod to your belief that people's insides count as much as the outsides. You'll mine till you find the diamond in everyone you meet.

Kick It Up TAKE-CHARGE, WISE, INTUITIVE   ***Step It Down*** OVERINVOLVED, UNDERSTATED

February 9

With its bright crystal studs, this Christian Louboutin "Maralena Flame" ankle boot blazes with a funky, fiery spirit that matches your own. An eternal optimist, holding the torch is your specialty. Like a renegade pep squad captain, you're the one who keeps people motivated about a mission from start to finish. Futuristic and inventive, this bootie could have been worn by a postmillennial Ziggy Stardust. You're no space cadet, but you have the ability to orbit beyond most people's realm of imagination. It's anyone's guess what you'll cook up in your lab next, but it's sure to be something both inventive and otherworldly.

Kick It Up INVENTIVE, MOTIVATING, FIERY   **Step It Down** OVERZEALOUS, UNYIELDING

February 10

The black petal segments of this Yves Saint Laurent "Jinny" suede wedge are stitched in a rainbow arc, evoking a strong element of femininity and fantasy. Like you, this shoe may have drifted straight from the fairy realm, a place where the ethereal comes to life. Here on Earth, you're a dream-keeper for many, encouraging loved ones to blossom and express their most imaginative ideas. Like the shoe's gilded trim, you may find yourself gravitating toward the upper echelons of society, but your spirit never becomes tarnished by materialism. You're charitable to the core, a patron of the arts, and one who believes in using money to make the world a better place.

Kick It Up CREATIVE, LUXE, CHARITABLE   **Step It Down** UNREALISTIC, DEMANDING

February 11

Half shearling boot, half leather sandal, this offbeat shoe runs the gamut from hot to cold. You're similarly versatile, not to mention as changeable as the weather. Your flights of fancy are manifold and have been known to carry you to the far corners of the Earth. Your loved ones need a GPS to keep up with you! You groove to a solidly bohemian beat, connecting to people wherever you go. You're a seeker in many realms, including the spiritual. Feathers, which adorn this shoe, are the symbol of ascension in many cultures—perfect for someone who is constantly evolving to higher planes of thought and existence.

Kick It Up ADVENTUROUS, SPONTANEOUS, WORLDLY   *Step It Down* ABSENT, DISCONNECTED

February 12

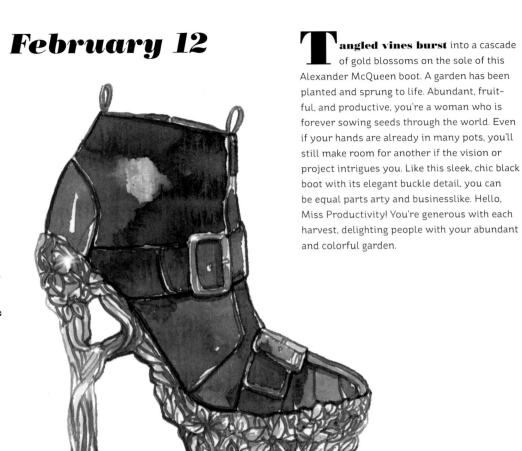

Tangled vines burst into a cascade of gold blossoms on the sole of this Alexander McQueen boot. A garden has been planted and sprung to life. Abundant, fruitful, and productive, you're a woman who is forever sowing seeds through the world. Even if your hands are already in many pots, you'll still make room for another if the vision or project intrigues you. Like this sleek, chic black boot with its elegant buckle detail, you can be equal parts arty and businesslike. Hello, Miss Productivity! You're generous with each harvest, delighting people with your abundant and colorful garden.

Kick It Up ABUNDANT, ACTIVE, CHIC   *Step It Down* OVERINVOLVED, HARSH

Bring on the Boogie Nights!

Like this 1970s platform disco sandal, your natural habitat is dead center on the dance floor. An unrepentant party girl, you know how to turn any occasion into a cause for celebration. Your wild side is matched by your rebellious streak: you'd rather sneak out the window than walk through the front door. It's just more fun that way! Like the shoe's glittering zigzag pattern, you move like lightning, flashing suddenly and changing course at a moment's notice. It's not that you mean to be erratic. You're simply far too interested in the world—and the people who inhabit it—to stay in one place for long.

February 13

Sign ★ AQUARIUS

Kick It Up DYNAMIC, ELEVATING, FUN   ***Step It Down*** INCONSISTENT, HEDONISTIC

February 14

"There is more hunger for love and appreciation in this world than for bread," said Mother Teresa. As a compassionate humanitarian, you understand this well. You believe that love is universal, and you have the ability to ignite that pure spark of connection with everyone you meet. With curves that evoke the shape of a heart, this 1950s Salvatore Ferragamo wedge mirrors your loving, uplifting nature. While you can be serious, you also have an irrepressible joie de vivre. Romantic and a tad decadent, the purple-and-gold fabric is as rich as your lust for life's most delicious pleasures and treasures.

Kick It Up COMPASSIONATE, HEARTFELT, JOYOUS   ***Step It Down*** GULLIBLE, WASTEFUL

February 15

You are a passionate idealist, here to transform the world into a place of equality for all. These historical suffragette boots are like those worn by Susan B. Anthony, who was born on this day. The leather shell is as tough as your stance, while the soft cloth button flap echoes your ability to be flexible in the name of progress. "Cautious, careful people, casting about to preserve their reputations . . . can never effect a reform," said Anthony. Whatever the cause you take up in this lifetime, you are willing to defy convention to create change—a true role model for all pioneering spirits!

Kick It Up IDEALISTIC, COURAGEOUS, PIONEERING   **Step It Down** BRUSQUE, COMBATIVE

February 16

A **conscious citizen of the world,** you believe in taking right action, voting with your dollar, and embracing the spirit of sustainability. You're a lover of all creatures great and small, with a special propensity for working with children and animals. These cutaway oxfords come from the socially responsible company Osborn Shoes, handmade by local artisans and workers in Guatemala. In addition to being in alignment with your ethos, the fabric is as bright and beautiful as your spirit. Transformation and rebirth are key themes in your life, and like the shoe's repurposed tribal cloth, you know how to make the old new again.

Kick It Up CONSCIENTIOUS, CARING, INGENIOUS   ***Step It Down*** RIGHTEOUS, STUBBORN

February 17

A **renegade explorer** and gypsy soul, you're at your happiest when you're roaming the world. Since you're fiercely independent, you're not afraid to make these treks on your own should your tribe be unable to accompany you. This nineteenth-century riding boot was worn by the nomadic Tatars, a breakaway group from the Near East that has migrated steadily for hundreds of years. The tooled leather pattern is gorgeously intricate, which speaks to your love of creating, understanding, and exploring life's complexities. Originality is a quality you prize highly. You're a collector of rare objects with a cultivated style that's all your own.

Sign ★ AQUARIUS

Kick It Up NOMADIC, ORIGINAL, INDEPENDENT   ***Step It Down*** ISOLATED, REBELLIOUS

February 18

"**Good girls go to heaven,** bad girls go everywhere," quipped *Cosmopolitan* editor Helen Gurley Brown, born on this day. Like the liberated media maven, you are a rebel in your own right, playfully defying convention and taking a stand for freedom. This Stella McCartney stiletto may be a soft petal pink, but its lines are sharp and in your face. Just as you'll take up a number of important causes in this lifetime, the toe of the shoe is stacked on an obvious platform. Naturally curious, you won't stop seeking until you find your answers. You know how to use your feminine wiles to disarm the opposition and get exactly what you need.

Kick It Up LIBERATED, VIVACIOUS, DEVOTED   *Step It Down* DEFIANT, NOSY

February 19

Bright and inquisitive, you are naturally curious about the world, but you are in no rush to figure everything out. The Victorian floral print on this Doc Martens boot is emblematic of your flowy, organic pace. You love taking time to stop and smell the roses, inhaling the sweet fragrance of each experience. Your passions tend to blossom quickly, and you're willing to work hard to cultivate your dreams. Like the treaded soles of this boot you have a sturdy, practical side as well. This bodes well on your numerous travels and adventures, many of which require a resilient attitude and a keen sense of humor.

Sign ★ AQUARIUS

Kick It Up INQUISITIVE, BOHEMIAN, TRAVELED   *Step It Down* SLOW-MOVING, DISTRACTED

February 20

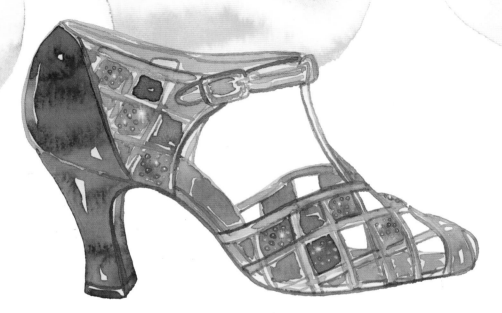

The iridescent lime-and-gold fabric of this 1935 Delman evening shoe could have been plucked from the feathers of a rare, exotic bird. You're an exceptional creature yourself, born with an innate understanding of human nature. With your keen memory, you can easily parrot back people's words and emotions, creating a vibe of rich understanding and acceptance. Few, if any, can mimic your spellbinding style. With your fanciful flights, your creativity is beyond compare. You're as deep and mesmerizing as the shoe's gem adornments, an enchanting mystery to behold.

Kick It Up EXOTIC, EMPATHETIC, MESMERIZING ***Step It Down*** DECEPTIVE, GUARDED

February 21

Intriguing, enigmatic, and captivating, you can't help but pique people's interest wherever you go. Like this Chanel bootie, you are class personified, coolly detached with a worldly air. Underneath that outer layer, you're a highly sensitive soul, which is why you often take such a self-protective stance. Here's a clue you share only with a chosen few: love brings out your softer side, which can be as warm and fuzzy as the shoe's bouclé accents.

Kick It Up INTRIGUING, CLASSY, CULTURED   ***Step It Down*** DEFENSIVE, COLD

February 22

Whimsical and romantic, you were born with stars in your eyes. You're a hopeless idealist, passionate about love, freedom, and your avant-garde principles. You may be earthbound, but only in physical form. These celestial-inspired platforms from Dolce and Gabbana are ready to lift you off to an alternate universe, a galaxy where your most vivid dreams might become a reality. Your passion burns as brightly as the shoe's red hue; your imagination glitters like its starburst of gems. When you're lit up with love, you're willing to leap without looking. Fortunately, you always land on your feet.

Kick It Up IDEALISTIC, PASSIONATE, BRIGHT   *Step It Down* CARELESS, DISCONNECTED

You are a sensible visionary who knows how to merge dreams and reality into an intoxicating cocktail. This Wellington-style boot from Vivienne Westwood keeps feet dry when splashing around in puddles. Its rich hue is poppy and fun, making it appropriate to wear rain or shine. You're similarly versatile, capable of weathering a broad range of elements and coming out with your upbeat attitude intact. Like the etched buttons, you leave a signature stamp on everything you touch, a glimmer of glamour that is simply unforgettable.

Kick It Up PRAGMATIC, CHEERFUL, ORIGINAL   *Step It Down* IMPENETRABLE, SUBDUED

February 24

Supportive and generous, you're at your happiest when you're helping other people improve their lives. This Christian Louboutin "Peace of Shoe" shares your mission. All proceeds from sales benefit microfinance opportunities in poverty-stricken nations. Give a girl a fish, she'll eat for a day. Teach her to fish, she'll dine for a lifetime. Although you're no stranger to sacrifice, it's best for you to take the latter route, empowering people by showing them the ropes. As sweet and feminine as the shoe's peony-pink hue, you view life through the lens of a romantic, always looking for the best in the people you meet.

Kick It Up CHARITABLE, EMPOWERING, SWEET ***Step It Down*** SACRIFICIAL, UNCLEAR

The gears of your mind are forever in motion, dreaming up brilliant notions, puzzling together mysteries, and otherwise engaging in intellectual ideas. Like this copper-brown Marc Jacobs wedge, you read as studious and somewhat under-stated. You're simply not the flashy type, preferring to be measured by the content of your character over anything else. Like the shoe's rubber sole, you have a spring in your step, especially when you're engaged in a project or relationship that challenges you to think outside the box.

Sign ★ PISCES

Kick It Up CEREBRAL, SINCERE, MODEST   *Step It Down* STARK, TIMID

February 26

This wedding slipper belonged to England's Queen Victoria, the longest-ruling female monarch in history. Like the queen, who married with her heart brimming with love, you are an unrepentant romantic. You'd walk to the ends of the Earth for your sweetheart, it's just that simple. During the Victorian era, peace, prosperity, and refined sensibilities were the order of the day. These are the hallmarks of your own realm. Your heart is pure, your predilections as sophisticated as the delicate ivory satin of this slipper. A natural leader, you rule with grace, warmth, and elegance.

Kick It Up LOVING, REFINED, GRACIOUS   *Step It Down* POMPOUS, MOODY

" I adore wearing gems, but not because they are mine," said Elizabeth Taylor, who was born on this day. "You can't possess radiance; you can only admire it." These dazzling evening pumps belonged to the legendary icon herself. With their silver detail, they sparkle and reflect, two of your greatest talents. Your brilliant presence has been known to light up a room. As a friend, you are an expert at mirroring people back to themselves, helping them see their own shining truths. Indeed, admiration is one of your most endearing traits. People feel like stars in their own right when they are walking the universe by your side.

Kick It Up INSIGHTFUL, BRILLIANT, SUPPORTIVE   *Step It Down* MIRED, PANDERING

February 28

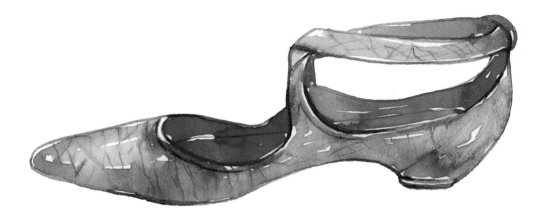

Where others see decay, you see character and beauty in its finest form. A transformer and alchemist, you are a master at breathing new life into the old. The cracked-bronze surface of this "Duke the Second" shoe from Irregular Choice mimics the peeling of a gilded *objet*. You never miss a flash of brilliance, especially one that's buried deep in the archives of the human soul. Falling in love with people's potential is something you do often. In your case, this is an absolute strength, since you are willing to work alongside others to help them cultivate their talents.

Kick It Up INTUITIVE, EXPERIMENTAL, ENCOURAGING   *Step It Down* IMPULSIVE, NAIVE

February 29

This Vivienne Westwood boot is printed in toile, the French fabric's pastoral scene reminiscent of the sweetness of yore. You're nostalgic by nature yourself, always looking for opportunities to bond in deep and intimate ways. Friends and family are your greatest treasure and the autobiography of your life reads like a cherished scrapbook of memories. Like the boot's elaborate textile, you are especially fond of details. It's not enough for you to hear a brief summary. You want full disclosure and can be quite a colorful storyteller yourself.

Sign ★ PISCES

Kick It Up SENTIMENTAL, DETAIL-ORIENTED, ENTERTAINING **Step It Down** RAMBLING, STUCK

February 20-March 19 *Pisces*

MARCH

March 20-April 20 *Aries*

March 1

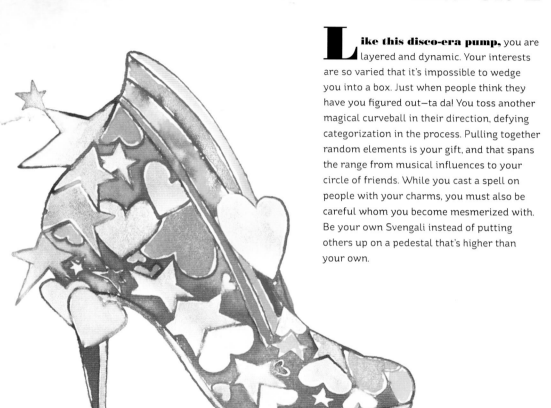

Like this disco-era pump, you are layered and dynamic. Your interests are so varied that it's impossible to wedge you into a box. Just when people think they have you figured out—ta da! You toss another magical curveball in their direction, defying categorization in the process. Pulling together random elements is your gift, and that spans the range from musical influences to your circle of friends. While you cast a spell on people with your charms, you must also be careful whom you become mesmerized with. Be your own Svengali instead of putting others up on a pedestal that's higher than your own.

Kick It Up WHIMSICAL, CREATIVE, ELECTRIFYING   ***Step It Down*** SCATTERED, BURNT OUT

March 2

A **mystic and an empath,** you are here to reveal the beauty of people's deepest emotions. You're not afraid to go deep, penetrating the superficial shell of human interactions with graceful ease. Your purpose in doing so? To truly understand people so you can lift them up to their highest potential. Like this Christian Dior feathered slingback stiletto, you seem to have emerged from the place where angels dwell. The jeweled detailing on the heel speaks to your fine-tuned attention to subtle nuances. You spot the gems that others miss, which is why people feel so understood in your presence. Conversely, there are very few who have the range to understand you, so when you find your soul circle of confidantes, keep them close for life.

Kick It Up COMPASSIONATE, SOULFUL, INTUITIVE   *Step It Down* CODEPENDENT, STUCK

Step to the side; the queen has arrived. You're far too powerful to be a princess, and like these elegant Miu Miu gold T-strap stilettos, you have a commanding grace about you. Although you don't mean to be intimidating, people can become so enchanted by your presence that they are afraid to approach you. This can leave you feeling lonely or isolated. While it will take some effort, turn down your sparkle from time to time to allow people a clear entry into your castle. Once they've crossed the moat, they'll enjoy basking in your benevolent glow, since your deepest desire is to share your abundant gifts with other people. A lifelong explorer, fill your royal court with scholars and healers who can guide you down the most positive of paths.

Kick It Up MAGNETIC, SEXY, POWERFUL *Step It Down* ISOLATED, UNAPPROACHABLE

March 4

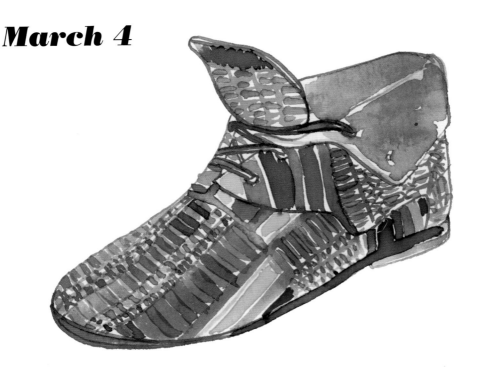

Revolutionary and dynamic, you are cut from a different cloth than most, much like this Osborn kente-print oxford. Guided by a vision for making the world a better place, you keep one eye on the future while simultaneously respecting time-honored customs and truths. You have an authoritative air about you, which makes you a shoe-in for most leadership positions. Power, however, is not something you're entirely comfortable with. The responsibility weighs on you, so like this soft, flat shoe, you prefer to be on the same level as the rest of the world. While the lace-up oxford style is thoroughly modern, the fabric holds the secrets of generations of indigenous women—a fusion of new and ancient that you exemplify.

Kick It Up REVOLUTIONARY, INNOVATIVE, COMMANDING   *Step It Down* RIGID, DICTATORIAL

A trusted confidante and keen intellectual, you're like the royal adviser to the king and queen; the person who is called upon when quick and creative solutions are needed. Like these gold metallic, high-top sneakers, you remain agile and brilliant when the rubber meets the road. While you are undeniably knowledgeable, it's not just book smarts with you. You draw from a deep wealth of firsthand experiences too. You aren't afraid to push yourself outside of your own comfort zone—especially when doing so provides an excellent learning opportunity. When it comes to your own private life, you don't give people easy access. Like the complex system of buckles and laces on this shoe, the ones who win your heart must be patient, smart, and fascinated by your complexities.

Kick It Up COURAGEOUS, EXPERIMENTAL, WISE   *Step It Down* SECRETIVE, ICY

March 6

Sign ★ PISCES

It's all romance all the time for you, a true believer in the power of love. Bring on the lacy, feminine flourishes like this Victorian-influenced lace ankle boot. The delicate perch of the stiletto heel decelerates your pace, helping you saunter along at just the right speed for people to stop and take notice of your vibrant persona. Do you love the attention? Well, if a valiant soul wants to sweep you off your feet and carry you over a puddle, thou doth not protest. Toes, never shown in true Victorian times because the foot was thought of as an erotic body part, peep out of this shoe, symbolizing your irrepressibly naughty streak.

Kick It Up ROMANTIC, IDEALISTIC, AUDACIOUS   *Step It Down* DEPENDENT, LANGUID

You're a renegade disco queen, grooving to the rhythm of your own mystic happy dance. Deeply spiritual and intuitive, you breeze through from the emotional realms without missing a beat. Bliss, you believe, is everyone's birthright. With your near-psychic sensibilities, you can literally feel people's pain, but you bring a unique ability to empathize, then energize, lifting people to the heights of ecstasy. Like this cotton candy–pink roller skate, you are capable of beaming joy and self-expression from every pore. Your wheels are always in motion, and you don't hit the brakes often. People need to catch you where they can, as you whiz from the French Riviera to Ibiza to the boardwalk of Venice Beach.

March 7

Sign ★ PISCES

Kick It Up BLISSFUL, ENLIGHTENED, ADVENTUROUS   ***Step It Down*** FLIGHTY, UNREALISTIC

March 8

Like this studded, lace-up bootie, you remain in perfect stride with the professional crowd and the party people. A paradox unto yourself, it's anyone's guess which side of your dualistic personality you'll display on any given day. To say you've got range is an understatement. You're both a rock star and the rock for your friends and family, a solid caretaker to the core. While you love your flash and glitz, you also require solid support, which the ankle height of this bootie provides. You're a little bossy . . . okay, more than a little, and the hints of dominatrix in this studded heel divulge your take-charge nature.

Kick It Up TAKE-CHARGE, MISCHIEVOUS, NURTURING   ***Step It Down*** DOMINEERING, STUBBORN

Now you see her, now you don't. Like the mermaid hiding behind the coral reefs, you are quiet, strong, and beautiful. While you certainly sparkle, you don't feel the need to be the flashiest one in the room. Just a glimmer will do, like the aqua iridescent leather and rhinestone toe embellishment of these vintage mules. Your subtle brand of glamour is reminiscent of the ladylike 1950s era, a time when clear Lucite found its place in footwear fashion. In the post–WWII era, the crystal-clear thermoplastic was a high-ticket item and the rage among the stylish set. Its translucence mirrors your occasional need to slip off to near-invisibility. You do your best work in private, and you simply must swim away when the siren's call of the muse rings in your ears.

Kick It Up ELEGANT, SELF-POSSESSED, INDEPENDENT   *Step It Down* EVASIVE, FLIGHTY

March 10

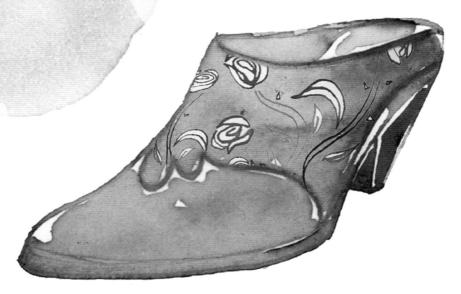

Like the clacking heel of this cowboy clog, you know that what goes up must always come down . . . and vice versa. This understanding of life's natural cycles is your ticket to freedom. You're not afraid to take chances—big ones—since you know that without risk, there can be no reward. If it doesn't work out, you'll just keep trying till it does. Criticism doesn't stop you in your tracks, since you're too busy playing and exploring to give much credence to the naysayers. Like this hybrid shoe, you're a little bit country and a little bit rock 'n' roll. You enjoy carrying on homespun traditions, but you always add your own individualized twist. There's a touch of a flower child in you, a dreamy idealist who wants life to be as sweet as a bed of roses.

Kick It Up UNSTOPPABLE, RELATABLE, SWEET *Step It Down* MISDIRECTED, WASTEFUL

Keen and innovative, you're a girl who likes being known for her smarts. You are an expert strategist, always thinking on your feet. Every choice you make is carefully considered, which is why the loafer, with its reputation for being such a sensible shoe, is your footwear alter ego. Geek chic is your calling card, but you also have your stylish street cred. With the dangling charm and unconventional color choice, this is not your librarian's loafer. With your casual style, you remain down to earth and can slip in and out of a variety of crowds without getting stuck in a clique. One of your deepest desires is to become a master of your craft, even if this takes a lifetime to achieve.

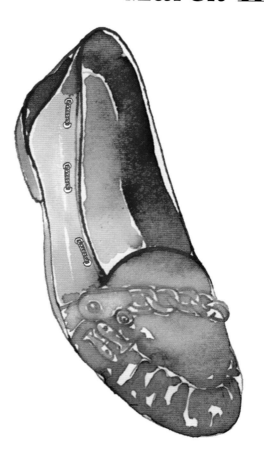

Sign ★ PISCES

Kick It Up SHARP, STRATEGIC, MASTERFUL ***Step It Down*** INTELLECTUALLY SUPERIOR, DETACHED

March 12

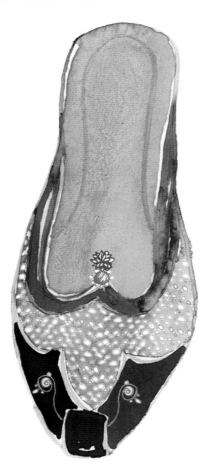

Like the shimmering hand-sewn detailing on this South Asian mojari, you lead a colorful, lavish, and adventurous life. Your view of the world could be described as kaleidoscopic. A traveler and a seeker, you are always in search of fresh perspectives. For you, there is no single truth, but endless fragments of reality, which, when pieced together, create a breathtaking and beautiful patchwork. Originally the domain of royalty, this enchanting slip-on is now sold in crowded markets, making finery accessible to the everyday person. While regal in aura, your ethos is decidedly grassroots. The richness of the human connection is far more precious to you than any status symbol, which is why you have friends from every walk of life.

Kick It Up BROAD-MINDED, WELCOMING, DAZZLING   *Step It Down* DISORIENTED, SUPERFICIAL

What's happening below the surface? That's the ever-present curiosity swirling through your mind. Like this mermaid-inspired Irregular Choice pump, you were designed for diving into mysterious waters and exploring the underworld. When you drift back up to the surface, you always make a splash, regaling people with your colorful and fantastic tales. The heel of this pump shimmers with the iridescence of an ocean nymph's tail, helping you find your land legs when standing on terra firma. That's a challenging task until you embrace your quirks instead of fighting them or hiding them. You might not swim with the mainstream school, but your visionary powers are needed above sea level.

March 13

Sign ★ PISCES

Kick It Up PENETRATING, ANALYTICAL, VERBOSE   *Step It Down* UNBALANCED, ISOLATED

March 14

Measured, thoughtful, and attentive, you are a keen observer of life. People-watching is one of your favorite activities, and this early 1900s spectator boot was designed for doing just that. Whether through the lens of a camera, a telescope, or your naked eye, you have a gift for discovering beauty in places where angels fear to tread. Communicating for people who can't find a voice may become your life's mission, making you an exceptional translator. You put a great deal of time and care into all that you do. That's why it's important for you to set your own pace instead of allowing others to hurry you along. When left to your own devices, you are an alchemist, turning what appears to be lead into shimmering gold.

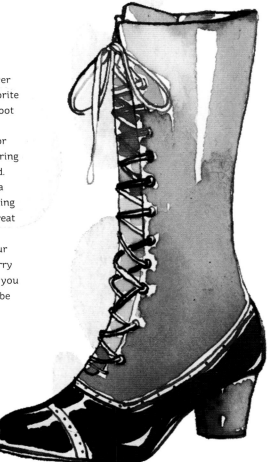

Kick It Up OBSERVANT, EMPATHETIC, SKILLFUL   *Step It Down* DEPRESSIVE, DETACHED

Calling all water nymphs! These sexy Vivienne Westwood peep-toes are made from rubber, giving you the ability to flow through H_2O in true Piscean style. With the alluring appeal of a Vargas pinup girl, you're a temptress and enchantress, casting a spell over everyone you meet. Like these poreless shoes, there is an impenetrable quality about you. Call it your protective outer shell; you are a highly sensitive individual, and it's all too easy for you to soak up other people's emotions. Your deepest desire is to become entwined with a soulmate, so when you finally find your other half, you give your heart for life.

Kick It Up SEXY, ENCHANTING, FLIRTATIOUS   *Step It Down* IMPENETRABLE, HYPERSENSITIVE

March 16

Anything boys can do, girls can do better: that could be your mantra. Like this trainer, you have a tomboyish edge, and woe betide anyone who tries to limit your capabilities. You're a hardworking woman who won't stop till she's reached the top. A star in your own right, you earn your stripes on merit, never expecting anyone to pull you up the ranks. Although you're imaginative, you keep a firm grip on reality, like these cleated soles. When there's a mission to accomplish, you jump right into the game, taking on a natural role as the captain of inspiration. Leading is something you do quietly, and by example rather than force.

Kick It Up HARDWORKING, INSPIRING, EXEMPLARY　　*Step It Down* CUTTHROAT, OVERLY MODEST

March 17

You dance on the edge of danger, the place where all true change begins. Life, as far as you're concerned, is far too short to waste time playing it safe. You'd rather stretch into the most daunting terrain, experiencing the thrills that come with each new experience. Like this thigh-high gladiator boot, you have the spirit of both a warrior and a badass. Some days you spiral up, others you spiral down, both with equal passion and fervor. Since you don't follow a predictable rhythm, you've been known to confound people. For those who love the chase, you're the ultimate challenge. Bound only to yourself, you won't be dominated, giving you the leg up over some incredibly powerful people.

Sign ★ PISCES

Kick It Up EXPLORATORY, UNDAUNTED, INDEPENDENT ***Step It Down*** ENIGMATIC, BELLIGERENT

March 18

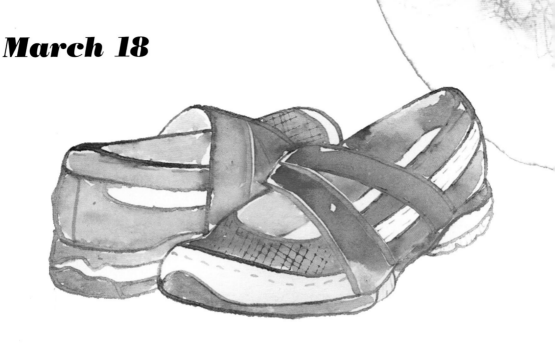

You're active and intuitive, with a wonderfully astute sense of timing. When the moment has come to make a move, you act without hesitation, surprising people with your speed and dexterity. With your keen understanding of interpersonal dynamics, you navigate through the toughest of situations, turning conflicts into win-wins. These Mary Jane sneakers have your feminine edge without falling into the girlie-girl category you flatly defy. Playful and a wee bit competitive, you get along just as well with the fellas as you do with the ladies. An expert negotiator, you love a good debate, but you also know when it's time to dim your fighting spirit and turn on your love light.

Kick It Up TAKE-CHARGE, ACTIVE, PLAYFUL   ***Step It Down*** RESENTFUL, MANIPULATIVE

Like these sequined 1960s mules, you have a timeless sparkle that cannot be repressed. You are radiant, magnetic, and ethereal, and people simply can't take their eyes off you—and, admittedly, you like it like that. Being the center of attention is a comfortable role for you, but never an ego trip. You are a magnanimous soul at heart. Once you are ensconced in the upper echelons, you love to use your privileged position to beam a light on other people's talents as well. Sequins, after all, are a reflective material. Glamorous and a little mysterious, you see life as an ongoing occasion to dress up and shine, both day and night.

Kick It Up MAGNANIMOUS, BEAMING, CAPTIVATING   *Step It Down* ELUSIVE, VAIN

March 20

Sign ★ ARIES

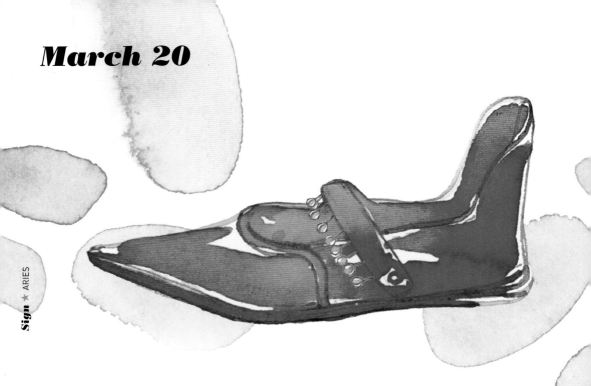

You are the first of the zodiac's warrior goddesses, fierce and fearless in your convictions. Eleanor of Aquitaine, who reigned as queen of both France and England during the Middle Ages, was a daring female crusader. She defied tradition, galloping on a white horse with an army of women. Beneath her armor, she may have worn this traditional medieval woman's shoe, which is more practical than embellished. Your royal presence needs no special announcement. You naturally ease into a role of authority and leadership because of your capable and sound judgment. Advising people at their most intense moments of transformation is one of your gifts. You're not afraid to fight for what you believe in, or to help others summon the courage to do the same.

Kick It Up FEARLESS, VALIANT, ONE OF A KIND   *Step It Down* DOMINATING, SELF-RIGHTEOUS

Born near the equinox, when day and night are of equal length, you are both a wide-eyed seeker and an old soul. These nineteenth-century leather slippers were crafted, in their time, to be worn at home after dusk. Today, with their elegant cutwork and embroidery, they would be stunningly appropriate when the sun is high in the noon sky. Similarly, you span quite a range, with a personality that's at once as deep as midnight blue and as feather-soft as buttercream. You pride yourself on being in the know: well read and well traveled, you are a citizen of the world who always maintains her strong sense of self, no matter where on the planet she decides to kick her heels up.

Kick It Up KNOWLEDGEABLE, DIVERSE, REFINED   *Step It Down* SUPERIOR, STUBBORN

March 22

Like a mad scientist, you're always up for fearless experimentation. Although your early efforts may seem far-fetched, your aim is always to produce something masterful. Undaunted, the world is your chemistry lab. You'll work tirelessly until you achieve your desired results, even if that means blowing up the beakers and starting from scratch over and over again. As Thomas Edison famously quipped, "I have not failed a thousand times. I have successfully discovered a thousand ways to *not* make a lightbulb." With your capable, can-do spirit, and your high-watt smile, this quirky, Chanel lightbulb heel is the perfect accompaniment to your "Eureka!" moment.

Kick It Up DYNAMIC, DIRECTED, ENTHUSIASTIC   **Step It Down** OVERBEARING, INSENSITIVE, PROUD

This serpentine stiletto is as elevated as your consciousness. A magnetic fireball, you carry age-old shamanic wisdom in your heart and soul. Traditions become transformational experiences under your careful tutelage. Forget about "just going through the motions." You help people connect the dots between thoughts and action so they understand the meaning behind all that they do. You are a fixer: Give you a mess, and you'll make it a masterpiece. People request the recipe to your secret brew, but you just can't explain it. Just as the mystical snake sheds its skin and regenerates, you are a master of the remix, inventing yourself anew after each rise and fall.

March 23

Sign ★ ARIES

Kick It Up TRANSFORMATIONAL, ELEVATED, WISE **Step It Down** TORMENTED, OBSESSIVE, EXTREME

March 24

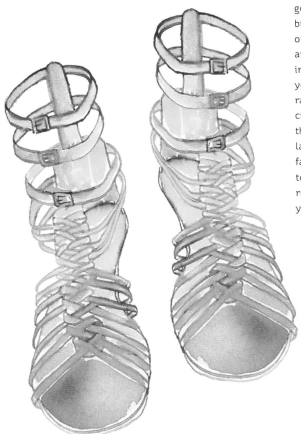

Like these Greco-Roman inspired sandals, you have the allure of a goddess. You're an icon of feminine power, bringing men to their knees with the charm of mighty Aphrodite herself. Enchanting and warm, you love life's pleasures and indulgences. You're a strong individual, but you prefer to work in partnership with others rather than to fly solo. You have a knack for creating win-wins, daring to unite elements that most people wouldn't think of mixing. The law of "opposites attract" always works in your favor. Here's a secret you might not admit to: you don't mind being the stronger one in relationships, and you have a tender spot in your heart for the softies.

Kick It Up CAPTIVATING, PERSUASIVE, ALERT *Step It Down* CONTROLLING, DIVALIKE

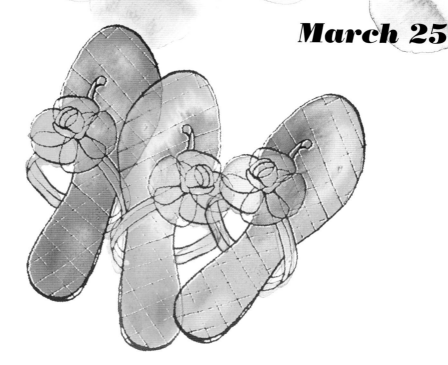

Candy sweet with a sassy streak, you're the chick that all the girls want to be. Like these adorable jelly flip-flops, you are accessible, chic, and inventive. It's not that you try to stand out from the crowd; you simply do. Although you often find yourself foisted up onto a pedestal, you're not too comfy way up there. You try to lead a transparent life, sharing yourself openly and allowing people to peek behind the curtain of your private affairs. With your multifaceted personality and wide-ranging interests, you need to slip in and out of different roles swiftly. Active and athletic, you seem to be in eternal motion, creating a colorful life with plenty of sparkle.

Kick It Up SASSY, ACCESSIBLE, INVENTIVE   **Step It Down** THIN-SKINNED, SCATTERED

March 26

You are a pillar of feminine strength and a tireless worker at that. Determined from the moment you take your first breath, you're here to achieve something meaningful and game changing. If that means fighting for a project, mission, or belief system, you're willing to jump into the fray without batting an eye. That's exactly why this twist on the combat boot is so you. Nobody's pushover, you're the one people want in their corner when it's time to negotiate. You're not signing on that dotted line until the terms are fair and favorable. Ultimately, this is in everyone's best interest, since you always pull your weight—and then some.

Kick It Up DETERMINED, FOCUSED, REVOLUTIONARY   ***Step It Down*** MILITANT, INFLEXIBLE

A **true original, you dance on the cutting edge,** much like history's first high heel. The Manchu chopine was the secret weapon of a Chinese army, dreamed up by Queen Duoluo Ganzhu to help soldiers trek through swampland and bypass the enemy troops. Like Ganzhu, you bring the fierceness of a warrior and the regal poise of a dynasty's figurehead. Where others may struggle to find balance, you stand firm and resolute. That's why people innately follow you, even though you're more than a few steps ahead of the game. Inevitably, your out-of-the-box ideas will elevate people to new realms of thought. Very few, however, can truly remain in step with you—which is why, on many days, you prefer to walk the world alone.

Kick It Up ORIGINAL, COMPETENT, GENIUS   *Step It Down* SELF-IMPORTANT, RECLUSIVE

March 28

Sign ★ ARIES

Shock jocks, step to the left! Like a bolt from the blue, you send tremors of astonishment through the crowds with your otherworldly moves. Your secret sauce always contains the element of surprise, but not in a destructive way. You're here to make life a magical and uplifting experience for everyone, from the party people in the ivory towers to the indie-fied underground set. Rather than reinventing the old, you'd rather start from the ground up, breaking from form like this heelless shoe. With your flamboyant personality, you draw stares and criticism regularly. It's par for the course for a trendsetter: you don't mind turning heads and shaking up the status quo.

Kick It Up ORIGINAL, AWE-INSPIRING, FEARLESS   *Step It Down* ATTENTION-SEEKING, INSINCERE

March 29

Like a true warrior princess, you're here to protect the innocent and uphold a sense of justice in your midst. Fittingly, this knee-high "Xena" boot is your ass-kicking alter ego in the footwear world. Although you're a firebrand, you believe in keeping a cool head and viewing life through an objective lens. "Live and let live" is your motto—as long as nobody steps on anyone's toes. While you're keenly aware of rules, you're fine with breaking them if it's for the greater good of the group. That renegade spirit can make people nervous at times, but they're always glad you're around to fight fire with fire.

Sign ★ ARIES

Kick It Up HONORABLE, DEVOTED, BRAVE ***Step It Down*** COMBATIVE, UNNERVING

March 30

Sign ★ ARIES

Vive la diva! You are an eminent empress who rises to her throne on the wings of her outsize talents. Like this crystal-encrusted sandal, you have an undeniably royal presence about you. Wealth, fame, and everything fabulous are your birthright, but you have to magnetize them to you. Keep on pushing yourself, even when you're afraid to take another step. By putting one foot in front of the other, you'll ultimately end up in the spotlight, which is exactly where you belong. Just don't forget the little people when your name is on the luminescent marquis.

Kick It Up BRILLIANT, REGAL, ENTERTAINING   *Step It Down* HAUGHTY, ELITIST

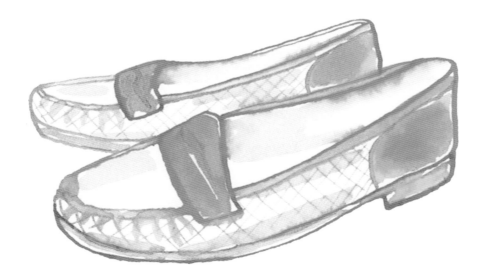

Like these colorful 1980s penny loafers, you have the ethos of the "me generation"—not because you are self-absorbed, but because you are self-assured. Your confidence inspires other people to take bold steps in their own lives. You are a born leader. Freedom is as important to you as authority. You'd rather collaborate with other independent spirits than have a fleet of subordinates reporting to you. Ultimately, you may wind up with the best of both worlds as people flock to be part of whatever party you're starting. Grounded and commanding, you know how to operate in a man's world and you always give the guys a run for their money.

Kick It Up CONFIDENT, COMPETENT, ASSURED *Step It Down* AGGRESSIVE, SOLITARY

Aries March 20 - April 20

APRIL

April 21 - May 21 Taurus

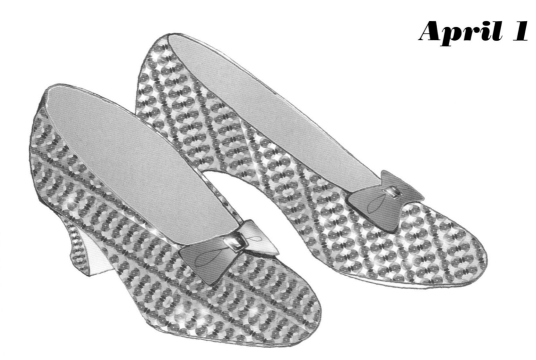

Yes! You do believe in magic—and with good reason. You've produced plenty of it yourself in this lifetime, always swooping in out of nowhere and taking people by surprise. As a lifelong adventuress, there's always somewhere over the rainbow you'd like to explore. These sparkly ruby slippers are the perfect accompaniment as you walk down life's proverbial Yellow Brick Road, collecting fascinating friends—and fans—every step of the way. Just click your heels together three times and visualize!

Kick It Up ADVENTUROUS, GREGARIOUS, SPARKLY   *Step It Down* MISGUIDED, FEARFUL

April 2

Sign ★ ARIES

You, like this purple wedge bootie, have your own enchanting formula for rising to new heights. It involves a dash of controversy, a splash of glamour, and a dollop of humor. With your razor-sharp observations, you always cut to the chase, pointing out areas in need of improvement. Sometimes this makes people angry, but being the contrarian type, you don't mind. You're tough enough to take it, knowing that in the end they'll be thanking you for helping them view the world from a more elevated place.

Kick It Up PRINCIPLED, ELEVATED, SHARP ***Step It Down*** ARGUMENTATIVE, STUBBORN

You're the Empress of Chic, a well-deserved position among your friends and peers. Like these vintage 1940s slippers, your casual elegance is both accessible and fanciful. Simply put, you're just fun to be around! While you consider life an ongoing occasion to celebrate, your inner wild child also needs room to roam. These slip-ons can kick off just as easily as they slide on when you need to venture down a rough-and-tumble path that few of your sisters have the nerve to navigate.

Sign ★ ARIES

Kick It Up ELEGANT, SELF-POSSESSED, ENTERTAINING   **Step It Down** REBELLIOUS, DISTRACTED

April 4

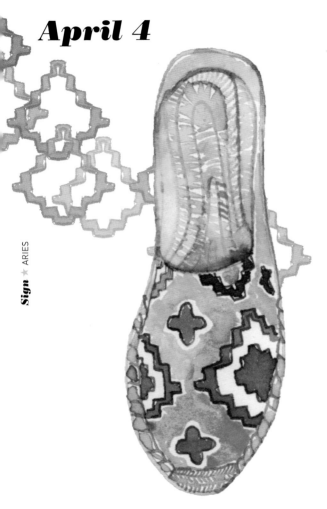

All God's Children Need Traveling Shoes is the title of Maya Angelou's autobiographical account of her years spent in Accra, Ghana. Like the poetess who shares your birthday, your quest for rich and meaningful experiences can lead you to the far corners of the globe. Worn from Bolivia to Bangladesh, this jute-soled woven espadrille is a staple for the intrepid journeyer like yourself. Relating to "the people" is more important to you than being high and mighty, although your visionary lens on life will eventually elevate you to a position of leadership.

Kick It Up DEEP, INTUITIVE, EXPLORATORY   **Step It Down** MELANCHOLY, FRUGAL

Like this updated twist on the 1950s saddle shoe, you might be sweet, but you pack a sassy punch. Originally worn as part of a school uniform, this shoe reflects your role as an eternal student of life. When it's time to rally for a meaningful mission, there's always plenty of pep in your step. People are often surprised by how quickly you raise your hand when someone is needed to take charge of a mission. Getting "saddled" with responsibility is something to look out for though, so learn the art of saying the graceful no.

Kick It Up GENEROUS, CURIOUS, OPEN   ***Step It Down*** NAIVE, OVERBURDENED

April 6

Who wants to paint the town crimson? The whimsical, cheery rhythm of the polka dot matches the upbeat tempo of your personality. You have a knack for seeing the opportunity in the most hopeless of circumstances, making you everyone's favorite goddess of inspiration. Your glass is not simply half full; it's overflowing. A true romantic, you can be unabashedly girlie when your heart is aflutter. Just like you, this sandal was made for picnics in the park, hand-in-hand strolls along the boardwalk, and long drives in convertible cruisers with the top down.

Kick It Up OPTIMISTIC, BUOYANT, ROMANTIC   *Step It Down* HEDONISTIC, DETACHED

Move over Sue Storm—there's a new action hero in town. Like this martial arts sneaker, you are ready to kick some ass when justice needs to be served. You walk softly, however, never meting out penalties that aren't merited. Your every move is measured and wisely calculated. When it's time to slip off into the shadows and observe people from a safe distance, you move with the stealth and grace of a panther. You also know when to turn on your veritable force field of energy—and whoa! People hardly know what hit them.

Kick It Up LOYAL, COURAGEOUS, FIERCE   *Step It Down* SUSPICIOUS, ALOOF

April 8

Blue velvet, the color of dusk, the symbol of intrigue, is lush and decadent. Like this sapphire-hued velvet Dior pump, you are elegant and mysterious. While you enjoy life's finer things, you are equally interested in exploring the hidden wisdom of the shadows—especially in the name of societal progress. With its innumerable threads, velvet refracts the light that shines upon it, glowing with a subtle luminescence. Similarly, your incandescent spirit can sometimes throw people for a loop. Where does your brilliance come from? You generally answer people with unexpected thoughts and ideas, illuminating philosophies that are way ahead of the curve.

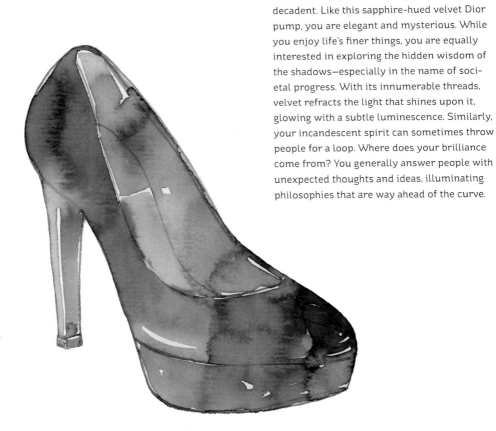

Kick It Up INTRIGUING, PROGRESSIVE, BRILLIANT   *Step It Down* CONTRARIAN, GUARDED

This rockabilly twist on a classic motorcycle boot shares your counterculture leanings without being overly obvious. The idea of being just like everyone else is foreign to you. By the same token, you never try too hard to be different. Uniqueness just appeals to you: it's a native form of self-expression rather than something to strive toward. Craftsmanship is something you value as well, and you'll strive tirelessly toward the mastery of one (or three) of your passions. A bit of a loner at times, you do your best work in the privacy of your own personal sanctuary.

Sign ★ ARIES

Kick It Up OFFBEAT, ORIGINAL, MASTERFUL   *Step It Down* STANDOFFISH, LONELY

April 10

You've got "star-studded" written all over you, like this Jeffrey Campbell "Lita" ankle boot. There's no doubt about it, you make a strong impression. Like the toughened-up vibe of this shoe, you are not one to be messed with. You love pushing the envelope and leading the charge, the self-appointed general of your own army. This is not just bravado: just as this boot folds over to reveal a studded layer, you are as fierce on the inside as you are on the outside.

Kick It Up FIERCE, STAR-POWERED, BRAVE   **Step It Down** AGGRESSIVE, ARROGANT

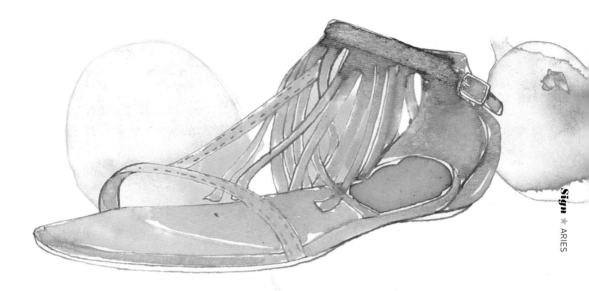

A soulful bohemian, you'd happily wander the Earth barefoot if you didn't get such a creative rush from your personal style. You love being on the fringe with your choices—fashion and otherwise—and this moccasin-style T-strap sandal keeps you right there. While you love your independence, you will ultimately need to surrender to your calling as a leader of your tribe. You leave far too inspiring a footprint to walk this Earth alone. Nevertheless, yours are definitely big shoes to fill!

Kick It Up FREE-SPIRITED, TRAILBLAZING, BOLD   *Step It Down* INTIMIDATING, COARSE

April 12

You're a true original—they broke the mold when they made you. The metallic snakeskin detailing and jewel-encrusted toe of this Miu Miu sneaker might normally be reserved for a collection of decadent evening shoes. On these sporty trainers, however, there's an element of shock value and in-your-face novelty—a perfect reflection of your untamed personality. Expressing yourself without restraint is what you're all about, even if that means stepping on people's toes from time to time. Besides, you're far too active to spend time tottering about on stilettos. You're in constant motion, and it's anyone's guess where you'll be found next, but you'll surely be marching to the beat of your own drum.

Kick It Up NOVEL, EXPRESSIVE, ADVENTUROUS   ***Step It Down*** REBELLIOUS, ARGUMENTATIVE

Oh, how expertly you charm, just like this beguiling snakeskin pump. The serpent, which sheds its skin each year, is surely your animal totem, as you are a master of renewal and transformation. For example: You're often the first to tout a novel idea or model a new style. You're also the first to leave these very strokes of genius behind, especially when a better invention comes along. Since you move at lightning speed, few can keep up with you. Like this peep-toe style, you know that revealing only parts of yourself is part of your enchanting mystique.

Sign ★ ARIES

Kick It Up TRANSFORMATIONAL, ALLURING, SPEEDY   **Step It Down** COMPLICATED, FICKLE

April 14

You're at once both a traditionalist and a progressive thinker—quite a paradox, but you manage to pull it off. Like this earthy clog, you have a dual purpose. Originally designed as protective footwear for workers, the clog evolved into a dancing shoe. At your core, you have a deep desire to shield your loved ones from harm. You'll fight to uphold your personal values, and can be quite a fierce contender in the ring. When it's time to celebrate, you shift gears quickly, becoming the life of the party, the central hub of the action, encouraging your flock to kick up their heels.

Kick It Up LOYAL, FIERCE, ETHICAL   *Step It Down* MORALISTIC, HEAVY-HANDED

April 15

Like the crimson hue of this Valentino pump, you have a bright and powerful presence that could literally stop traffic. Intensely physical, you understand how to use movement and body language to create a lasting impact. You arch and dance like the shoe's sculptural bow, stirring up excitement and energy in anyone who lays eyes on you. With your va-va-voom flair, you're sexy without having to try, but you bear no scarlet letter. You're as principled as you are vivacious, a mix that leaves you well respected and in the driver's seat at all times.

Sign ★ ARIES

Kick It Up IMPACTFUL, VIVACIOUS, IMPRESSIVE   *Step It Down* OVERPOWERING, RACY

April 16

Around and around and around you go. Like the unique corkscrew heel of this sandal, your life is a dramatic spiral of events. This is by design, of course, since anything too predictable simply bores you. As you ride the proverbial merry-go-round, you learn your most important lesson: nothing is permanent, except change. Regardless of your ephemeral nature, you are capable of getting attached to people, especially those who are as eager to take on challenges as you are.

Kick It Up INVENTIVE, UNDAUNTED, FUN   **Step It Down** RESTLESS, UNGROUNDED

The bow ties embellishing this Chanel mesh bootie evoke the formal elegance of a tuxedo. For you, every day is a meaningful occasion, and you live life with a strong sense of purpose. As the expression goes, "Want something done right? Give it to a busy person." That would be you. Innovative and ambitious, if you don't have a reason to dress up, you're bound to create one. Like the shoe's airy mesh panels and streamlined heel, you remain light on your feet at all times—even when tackling challenges that most people would find daunting.

Kick It Up MOTIVATED, SOPHISTICATED, PURPOSEFUL   *Step It Down* OVERZEALOUS, OFFICIOUS

April 18

Red: the signature Aries hue and the color often associated with aristocracy. In the seventeenth century, France's king Louis XIV declared that only those who had curried royal favor were allowed the privilege of donning crimson-colored heels. While you're definitely not down with the French king's pomp and circumstance, there is something undeniably regal about you. When you step into a room, people know that someone important has arrived—someone so loving and gracious that they'd gladly exalt her to the throne.

Kick It Up REGAL, CARING, BENEFICENT   ***Step It Down*** INSECURE, OVERLY FORMAL

April 19

With your sunshine-bright disposition, people can't help but fall under your cheery spell. Like this beachy, cork-heel slip-on, you have a casual allure that is far more inviting than it is intimidating. In many ways, you're wired like a California beach bunny, ready to dive into the fun the moment she hears that the surf's up. The one major difference: your free-spirited nature is matched by an awe-inspiring serious streak. You'll never shy away from daunting responsibilities, especially if they bring the promise of building a nest egg for your dearly beloved.

Sign ★ ARIES

Kick It Up OPTIMISTIC, DETERMINED, INVITING   *Step It Down* FLAKY, CARELESS

April 20

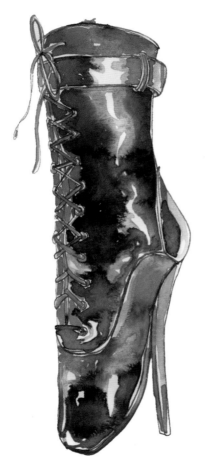

This fetishwear ballerina boot is not for the faint of heart nor the Average Jane. It takes deft skill to arch the foot to a dancer's curve, and once laced in, little mobility can be achieved. Endurance, skill, and strength are required—three of your most stellar traits. Like this shoe, you are not bound by convention nor drawn to the conventional. Your resilience allows you to stand tall and firm where others may topple under pressure. Because you are such a powerful force of nature, people often confess they feel intimidated by you. This surprises you every time, as you're not always aware of your own might.

Kick It Up SKILLED, RESILIENT, EXTRAORDINARY   *Step It Down* DOMINATING, INTIMIDATING

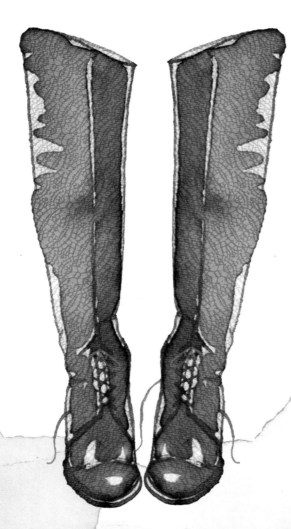

April 21

Whether you're jumping over fences or jumping through hoops, you'll do whatever it takes to bring your dreams to the finish line. While you'll happily canter along a gentle trail, you don't mind riding through rough terrain when you have your eyes on the prize. This sleek, tall pair of equestrian boots keeps you firmly planted on your saddle as you gallop off on the hunt. Classic and understated, these boots don't need to announce themselves in an obvious way. Nor do you, as your timelessly chic style always commands respect.

Sign ★ TAURUS

Kick It Up CHIC, STRONG-WILLED, AMBITIOUS   **Step It Down** POWER-HUNGRY, SNOBBISH

April 22

Sign ★ TAURUS

Let's get one thing clear: you are here to run the show. You rarely arrive without a battle plan in place, and the troops quickly fall in line under your capable governance. This vamped-up twist on the military boot heralds itself with authority and sex appeal, just like you. A tireless overachiever (who somehow always appears fresh), you accomplish in minutes what takes others hours to pull off. What do you want, a medal or something? Well, yes. Isn't that obvious? You were born to be a decorated member of society, collecting merit awards and trophies throughout the years.

Kick It Up EMPOWERING, VISIONARY, FEARLESS   ***Step It Down*** OVERACHIEVING, MILITANT

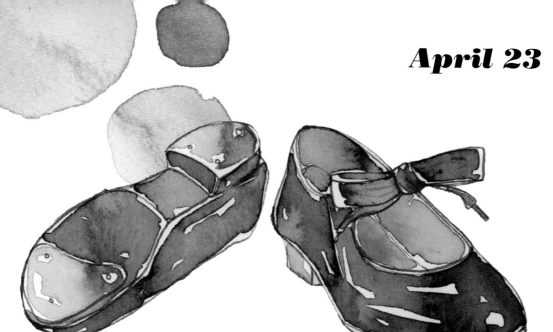

Tap, tap, tap. With your steadfast devotion, you keep the beat for the people in your universe. You groove to a complex rhythm, but you are a grounded person to the core. Resilient, innovative, and loyal, you are here to learn, master, and uphold traditions. Somehow you manage to be at once a bossypants and a total sweetheart—and that's no easy line to walk. It's your girlish charm that, like these adorable tap-dancing shoes, makes people buckle under your spell.

Kick It Up ANIMATED, ENDEARING, GROUNDED *Step It Down* BOSSY, STUBBORN

April 24

Like this bejeweled ballet flat, you love to sparkle, but your nature is essentially practical. You're a bit of a "mother superior" type, nurturing the people in your midst and empowering them to be their best. You're also a glamour-puss, and like the reflective jewels on this slip-on, you are here to mirror people's best back to them—and occasionally their worst. You're not afraid to dole out the tough love when you know it's needed. Your direct communication style might make some balk, but people never question the fact that you truly do care.

Kick It Up NURTURING, SUPPORTIVE, GLAMOROUS ***Step It Down*** NAGGING, OVERBURDENED

April 25

"**I**magination will often carry us to worlds that never were. But without it we go nowhere," said astronomer Carl Sagan. Fortunately, you're no stranger to *le voyage fantastique*. With your vivid imagination and endless curiosity, you live a life that's as dreamy and as colorful as the swirl of this Christian Dior platform. The woven espadrille heel and bold red bow give the shoe a sporty, casual feel. Similarly, you're equal parts ethereal and down to earth, pulling off practical plans with surprising ease. No wonder people find you tough to categorize. You can be a whole lot to handle when you fan your feathers, but toning it down is just not an option for you.

Sign ★ TAURUS

Kick It Up CURIOUS, DREAMY, DYNAMIC   ***Step It Down*** CONFUSING, OSTENTATIOUS

April 26

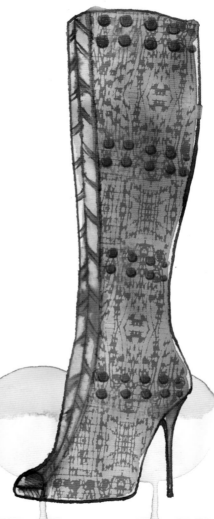

Like the repeating weave of this Gucci peep-toe boot, you understand the power of patterns and how the parts of a whole all weave together. Efficient and organized, you are an expert at creating new systems and decoding the ones that exist. Just as these boots trail high up the leg, you will go to great lengths to figure out a problem that is puzzling you. Friends and family come to you regularly for a dose of practical magic and a solution from your arsenal of earthy wisdom. Like the natural hue of the boot, you don't need to be the flashiest person in the room to make a powerful statement.

Sign ★ TAURUS

Kick It Up EFFICIENT, RESOURCEFUL, WISE   *Step It Down* INFLEXIBLE, SEVERE

Padukas are India's oldest shoes, initially worn by religious devotees. Although simple in construction, they require focus and willpower to wear them, since the toe-knob must be gripped to keep the shoe on the foot. As a highly principled person, you have a strong grasp on your values and ideals. You will clutch to your beliefs, even in the face of a daunting challenge. Early padukas were fashioned from wood, but with your taste for life's luxuries, this silver pair is more befitting. Adorned with small bells, this type of paduka is given as gifts and is used in ritual celebrations to this day.

Kick It Up STRONG-WILLED, LUXURIOUS, PRINCIPLED   *Step It Down* STRICT, HOLIER-THAN-THOU

April 28

You are radiant and compelling, and people are simply magnetized to you. Like the generous cutaways of this rose-gold Ferragamo sandal, you are willing to reveal a lot about your life, particularly the lessons you've learned from your hardships. Your authenticity inspires trust in others, who see you as a role model. Still, you can be deeply mysterious, especially when in the heart of a struggle. You prefer to work out your issues in private, veiled like the curtain of chains dangling from this stiletto's strap. Fortunately, you always emerge with wisdom to bestow, and you may even write or speak publicly about your experiences in this lifetime.

Kick It Up AUTHENTIC, INSPIRING, MAGNETIC   ***Step It Down*** PROUD, SUPERIOR

Like this Kate Spade "Becca" flat, you are a vibrant soul who knows how to make a splash without being garish or ostentatious. People sit up straight when you step into the room, since you carry yourself with grace and confidence. The gleaming jeweled pendant embellishing the shoe's toe echoes your love of fine luxuries—and your attraction to elite circles of people. Like the chocolate-brown bow, you never leave loose ends dangling. Everything you do is tied up neatly, which is why so many people depend on you to get the job done right.

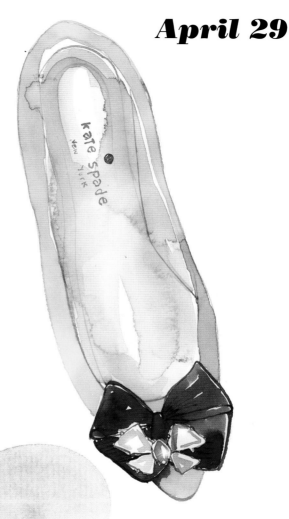

Sign ★ TAURUS

Kick It Up CHIC, DEPENDABLE, GRACIOUS   ***Step It Down*** ELITIST, CONTROLLED

April 30

What appears black and white on the surface is never as elementary as it seems. In any given situation, you are able to find the gray area without disrupting the striking contrast of dark and light. With its chunky sole, these 1938 vintage Ferragamo sandals have a solid presence. Similarly, you thrive in an environment that is stable and structured. Yet you're no Goody Two-Shoes. Once you understand the rules, you flow with them artfully, like the curvy brocade accenting the shoe's heel. Parameters that may feel rigid to other people only spur you on to be more imaginative—you're a genius at discovering intricacies within the most pared-down circumstances.

Kick It Up STRUCTURED, IMAGINATIVE, GENIUS   *Step It Down* STUBBORN, HEAVY-HANDED

Taurus April 21-May 21

MAY

May 22-June 21 **Gemini**

May 1

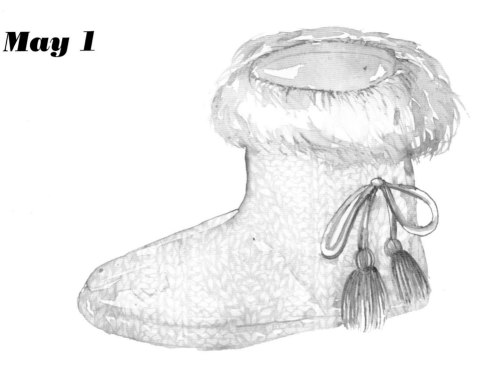

Sensual and comfort loving, you require footwear that feels as good as it looks. This fur-lined slipper meets your need for such luxury while giving you carte blanche access to kick back and relax. More a leader than a follower, you prefer your treasures to be one of a kind. The intricate knit of these slippers sets them apart from the off-the-shelf pack, while the undyed yarn appeals to your earth sign sensibilities. Now brew up a pot of tea, relax with a thick novel, and escape to another world.

Kick It Up LUXURIOUS, PERCEPTIVE, UNIQUE   ***Step It Down*** OVERINDULGENT, LETHARGIC

Structured and stable, you like to look before you leap. By no means does that require you to walk through life in boring "sensible shoes." Form can follow function *wand* be fashionable: this truth you hold to be self-evident. Ladylike and chic, this stacked, architectural pump keeps your heel elevated to a walkable angle as you jet from one meeting to the next. The geometric pattern echoes your sharp and linear thought process. When it's time to cut to the chase, there's no better leader than you!

Sign ★ TAURUS

Kick It Up STABLE, SHARP, CHIC   ***Step It Down*** SEVERE, CUTTING

May 3

Sign ★ TAURUS

You might be a hard-nosed realist, but you're still a colorful character. Like this Gucci cutaway sandal, you know how to balance the weighty with the bright. The classic black strap has the feel of timeless elegance, but juxtaposed against cobalt and aqua, it becomes part of a more playful story. Similarly, you can swing between society lady and party girl without batting an eye. You dance on the line of propriety, rarely crossing into rebel territory, but certainly willing to push people's buttons if it means making the world a better place for all its inhabitants.

Kick It Up BRIGHT, CHARITABLE, RELIABLE   *Step It Down* TOUGH, DISAPPROVING

Like the tweed fabric adorning this pump, you are at once both homespun and businesslike. It's not your desire to be the center of attention, but rather a Best Supporting Actress who makes sure that everyone's greatness is showcased. Your nurturing nature dovetails beautifully with your crisp professionalism. On an average day, you dole out warm hugs and firm edicts in equal measure. The kitten heel appropriately softens your edge while making it clear that you are not one who can easily be pushed over. When it comes to defending your principles or standing up for the ones you love, you'll dig your heels in until your voice has been heard.

Kick It Up PROFESSIONAL, NURTURING, PROTECTIVE   ***Step It Down*** STERN, CONVENTIONAL

May 5

This hot-pink python pump from Vivienne Westwood announces itself boldly. "We have arrived," it seems to say. "The party may now begin." You bring a similar electric charge to any room you step into. Things just start to percolate when you're around. You enjoy being the authority on matters and can even be a bit of a know-it-all at times. Like the weighty platform of this pump, you are not one who is easily moved from her stance. Nevertheless, you remain graceful, arching elegantly through conflict like the rounded curve underneath the carriage of this exotic shoe.

Kick It Up KNOWLEDGEABLE, ASSERTIVE, ENERGETIC   *Step It Down* OVERBEARING, WILLFUL

The oxford meets the Mary Jane here, giving way to an unexpected mashup of dressy formality and girlish surprise. These gender-blending shoes echo your own ability to walk powerfully among women and stay in stride with the traditional "man's world." You like to keep a foot in both camps, managing to be flirty without coming across as flighty, professional without being pedestrian. Indeed you have a smile that could launch a thousand ships, but your nature is too charitable to send people to war. You'd rather send supplies overseas to feed the hungry or rebuild a war-torn nation: missions you might just spearhead before your life is through.

Kick It Up CHARITABLE, PROACTIVE, ENTICING   *Step It Down* MISLEADING, ACCOMMODATING

May 7

This black lace-up heel—inspired by traditional Irish dance gillies—evokes a masterful yet fluid style. Graceful and determined, you appear unruffled on the surface, but this belies your hidden skill. There's great care, thought, and a sense of purpose behind every move you make. Irish dance is steeped in heritage, and you can be a traditionalist in many ways. You aren't afraid to modernize customs, however, like this fashion-forward spin on what is normally a fairly plain shoe. Inventing new ways to celebrate your lineage can be a rich and rewarding experience to you and your dearly loved family.

Kick It Up FLUID, SKILLED, EAGER TO LEARN   **Step It Down** CLIQUISH, OVEREXTENDED

Pass the petition, the picket sign, and the stack of pamphlets. With your high-minded vision and huge heart, you're ready to rally for a cause at a moment's notice. A stellar organizer, you're often at the helm of humanitarian missions. As a product of TOMS, these shoes are a fashionable incentive to do good in the world. With every pair of TOMS shoes purchased, a new pair of shoes is donated to a child in need—a cause that's bound to put a spring in your altruistic step.

Kick It Up ENERGETIC, ORGANIZED, PRINCIPLED   *Step It Down* PUSHY, IN-YOUR-FACE

May 9

Timeless elegance is your calling card, like this chic and classic pump. You realize that trends may come and go, but certain truths remain etched in stone as the years go by. A highly principled person, you're here to uphold ethical standards and long-standing values. If a time-honored tradition is going to be changed, there better be a darn good reason for it. Like the squared-off toe, you can have a blunt edge. Your matter-of-fact cool can be intimidating, but ultimately you command respect as you stand firmly for what you believe in.

Kick It Up TIMELESS, RESPECTED, CHIC   **Step It Down** RIGID, MORALISTIC

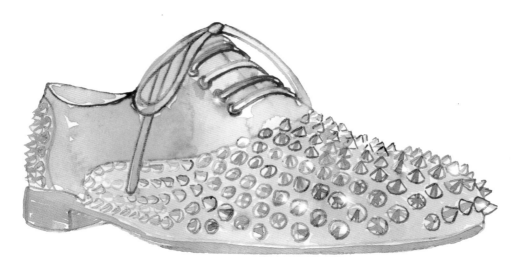

Edgy, opinionated, and willing to go against the grain, there's a bit of a punk rock girl in you. This studded Louboutin oxford exemplifies your rebelliousness. Indeed, you've intimidated a few souls in your day. Underneath your somewhat aggressive exterior beats the heart of a devoted confidante. As a friend, there's no one more loyal than you—and you're always willing to go the distance for the ones you love. Your alone time is precious to you too, so give yourself permission to break away from your friends.

Kick It Up LOYAL, INDIVIDUALISTIC, ORIGINAL   **Step It Down** ANTAGONISTIC, GUARDED

May 11

Hello, Twinkletoes. This gold T-strap pump makes a sparkly statement with each step, just as your personality sprinkles pixie dust over all who come into your sphere. Ornate, but never gaudy, you are the walking definition of festive refinement. You believe that life should be shared and celebrated with wonderful people as often as possible. You are a superconductor of electrifying personalities and magical beings, who you seem to meet at every turn. As such, you often find yourself choreographing large gatherings around your magnificent hearth.

Kick It Up REFINED, ENCHANTING, FESTIVE   *Step It Down* OVERCOMMITTED, FICKLE

Sign ★ TAURUS

Your impish nature finds its fair footing in these elf-inspired slip-ons. Although you may read as somewhat serious on the surface, there's an undeniable twinkle in your eye. Your sense of humor is smart and slow to unfold. Because of your ability to keep a poker face, you're often the last person to be pinpointed as the jokester. Ha ha! This only makes your follies ten times funnier. While you live to laugh, you're also a person of great substance. Grounded and capable of juggling numerous responsibilities, you're as trustworthy as they come. Humor, however, helps you whistle through your work.

Kick It Up COMICAL, CAPABLE, CLEVER   **Step It Down** SNEAKY, MISLEADING

May 13

Cue the Aretha Franklin. Shoes that make you feel like a "natural woman" are your ideal fit. You're constantly evolving to the next level, through your studied connection to the Earth, your environment, and the people who inhabit it. These woven ballet flats made from undyed fibers appeal to your "keep it simple" ethos. Too many bells and whistles just slow you down. With your nomadic nature, it's anyone's guess where you'll kick up your feet next. You might be dancing at an international festival with other free spirits, winding your way through a bazaar, or peering at rare birds through a pair of high-powered binoculars.

Kick It Up SINCERE, MOTIVATED, CURIOUS   **Step It Down** UNPREDICTABLE, DISTRACTED

Ready, set, go! Motivated by ideas and fueled by adrenaline, you're ready to dash out of the gates the moment genius strikes—which, in your case, is often. Few can keep up with your mercurial mad dash. You, however, refuse to slow down. This aerodynamic sneaker is your "sole mate" in the shoe world, and if a rocket booster were sold separately, you'd be sure to affix it to the heel. For the time being, you'll have to settle for the spring-action lift and the power of kinetic energy.

Kick It Up ENERGETIC, INSPIRED, DRIVEN   *Step It Down* RASH, WASTEFUL

May 15

Naughty or nice? You'll take a large helping of both, thank you very much. Like this "I Do" peep-toe from Seychelles, you can appear to be as pure as the driven snow. The pretty, sexy cutaways belie any rumors of primness, however. Once you decide to unlace your formal outer shell, there's a bit of a wild child inside. You rely on the element of surprise to create magic in the world—it's one of your most enchanting superpowers. Resourceful and partnership oriented, you like to create win-wins with people, turning what already exists into an upcycled masterpiece.

Kick It Up MYSTICAL, SURPRISING, RESOURCEFUL   ***Step It Down*** SECRETIVE, MORALISTIC

Like this glitter-heeled suede Christian Louboutin platform, there's a sparkle in your step—not to mention a mischievous twinkle in your eye. Impishly irresistible, you lead the charge among your friends when it comes to having fun. With its chunky sole and bubbly shape, this is not a shoe that takes itself too seriously. Nor do you. Life without laughter is an empty proposition to you. Nevertheless, you are still a solid citizen. There's a weighty durability to this sandal, just as your friends and family know you to be a dependable soul whom they can rely on.

Kick It Up IMPISH, HUMOROUS, DEPENDABLE   *Step It Down* TROUBLEMAKING, CALLOUS

May 17

Sign ★ TAURUS

What appears to be simple is never quite that. The beginnings of this Alexander McQueen basic black boot have been cut, studded, laced, and reconfigured—it's not simple to get into this shoe. That's how you roll: not just anyone can enter your somewhat private universe. You're a bit guarded and, at times, bound up in mystery. Once you decide to grant people access, however, you stick by them till the bitter end. The complex corners of the universe are your preferred stomping grounds. Anything (or anyone) that fits too neatly into a predetermined category will not hold your attention for long.

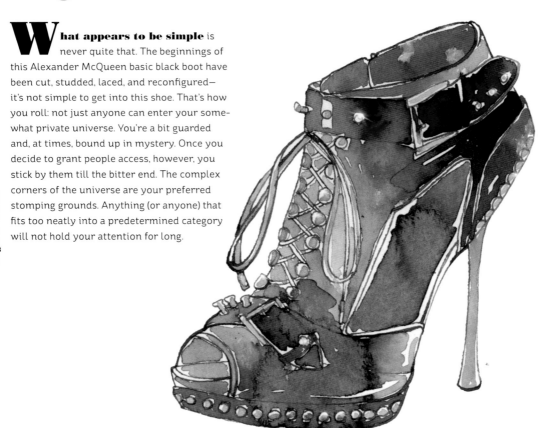

Kick It Up MULTIFACETED, LOYAL, INTRIGUING   **_Step It Down_** ENIGMATIC, UNFRIENDLY

Let your voice be heard! Candid and cause driven, you can be unabashedly vocal when you see the need for change. Practical progress is what you believe in. You're not here to rock the boat, but rather to steer it in the most useful direction. This sandal is the ideal accoutrement for your campaigning efforts: comfortable, casual, and down to earth. With your feet fixed firmly on the ground, you can delight in your bohemian rhapsody while enjoying your role as a responsible citizen of planet Earth.

Kick It Up OUTSPOKEN, CARING, PRACTICAL   *Step It Down* IMMOBILE, RIGHTEOUS

May 19

Some things are best seen in black and white, like this luxe zebra-striped ankle boot. While you're willing to color outside the lines, you also know how to cut straight to the chase. Blunt? Fierce? Hopelessly uncensored? You can be all of the above. Nevertheless, your hard-hitting edge is part of your charm, and your wild nature is as delightful as it is daunting. You are clearly not a person to be messed with, so anyone who dares defy you better bring a strong argument. One way or another, you are determined to get your way.

Sign ★ TAURUS

Kick It Up FEARLESS, DYNAMIC, FIERCE   ***Step It Down*** CUTTING, AGGRESSIVE

May 20

Extroverted doesn't even begin to describe you. Like the spiky strap of Christian Louboutin's "Rodarte" platform Mary Jane, you radiate outward-flowing energy from every pore. Some may accuse you of being an exhibitionist. You won't deny it. You're in your element when you're shining and sparkling before a crowd. You're not afraid of heights, and like the reflective surface of this stiletto, you move at the speed of light. It's important for you to slow down at times so you don't fall off balance. Since you're not always aware of your own maximum limits, having a nurturing support circle is a must.

Sign ★ TAURUS

Kick It Up OUTGOING, DAZZLING, UNSTOPPABLE   **Step It Down** OSTENTATIOUS, BURNT OUT

May 21

Some might call you bossy, but you just have . . . a vision. And it's a vision that you intend to take to the finish line, no matter what the obstacle. This sky-high stiletto in "I mean business" black commands authority while remaining staunchly sophisticated. You could move mountains with sheer will, but that's hardly necessary. A gifted, empowered, and dynamic leader, you are at your best in the role of director, delegating tasks to people who are eager to learn from you. Patience, however, is not your strong suit, so you may need to summon a second in command to help you deal with the aggravating details of daily life.

Kick It Up DETERMINED, POWERFUL, SOPHISTICATED   *Step It Down* MANIPULATIVE, IMPATIENT

Some people fear the unknown. You embrace it, wide eyed, active, and eager to learn. The world is your playground, and you want to explore every corner of it. These purple metallic high-tops repeat your flash and movement. You're a head turner, but you're also accessible to other people. Socially, you enjoy bonding with people from all walks of life, but your preference is for those who aren't afraid to walk an unconventional path. These creative souls are your muses, inspiring you to dream in bright colors and to put your most daring foot forward.

Kick It Up PLAYFUL, UNCONVENTIONAL, CREATIVE   *Step It Down* SUPERFICIAL, RECKLESS

May 23

Sign ★ GEMINI

"**Heart and head** are the constituent parts of character," said Casanova. Indeed you are deeply connected to both cranium and *corazón*, which makes you not only a well-rounded soul, but a wise adviser as well. Your logical mind fires off thoughts at lightning speed. Your heart charges you up with emotion with every beat. This Badgley Mischka "Randee" sandal walks the same line. The alluring chiffon rose softens the shoe's clean, classic lines, striking a balance that is chic, sexy, and smart. Poetry in motion, just like you!

Kick It Up INTELLIGENT, COMPASSIONATE, ALLURING   ***Step It Down*** VAIN, DISTRACTED

May 24

Like this platform go-go boot, you take an elevated perspective on life. You tend to walk the high road, but figuring out where that path lies can be quite a journey for you. Just as the great seekers throughout history hypothesized complex theories for their time, your thoughts are often in a swirl as you ponder this angle and that point of view. Indeed, you enjoy the process of thinking things through as much (if not more than) the end result. Like the dual-toned leather of these boots, you like to have at least two options to weigh before you make any decision.

Sign ★ GEMINI

Kick It Up HIGH-MINDED, CURIOUS, INTELLECTUAL **Step It Down** CLOUDED, INDECISIVE

May 25

Life is not a spectator sport—nope, not in your universe. Like this Roman gladiator, you are always ready to jump into the ring and show off your skills. Some may find you combative, but you're just having fun. For the original wearers of the gladiator sandals, fighting was a form of entertainment. A bit of a contrarian, you enjoy a spirited debate and a verbal sparring session. Pushing people's buttons amuses you, although you sometimes take things a bit too far. Fortunately, you have a compassionate streak to match your impish one, and you can always rely on your humor to get you out of a jam.

Kick It Up SPIRITED, ENTERTAINING, HUMOROUS ***Step It Down*** COMBATIVE, INSENSITIVE

What's life without a little contradiction? Like the peep-toes of these Alexander Wang booties, you're willing to reveal plenty of information about yourself. But just when people think they've got you pegged, surprise! A hidden layer is revealed, like the one that lies below the shoe's zipper. Versatile and mutable, you're capable of walking in two very distinct worlds. You can be as signature All American as these denim panels when you choose to fit in with the crowd. When your fierce side is ready to play, out comes the bad girl, who will jump in the ring and fight for what she believes in against the most formidable opponents.

Kick It Up VERSATILE, MULTIDIMENSIONAL, EXCITING   *Step It Down* AGGRESSIVE, DUPLICITOUS

May 27

Pick a lane! Although you're a capable multitasker, when you focus on a single path, you score in a big, big way. These Adidas bowling shoes are the footwear of choice for the focused game you are here to play. Although the actions of your craft may seem repetitive, there's an artful dance involved. Becoming a master of the subtle details is the key to your life's work. There's a dash of panache in the design of the bowling shoe, which is why they're embraced by die-hard competitors and hipsters alike. Similarly, you possess both intellect and the cool factor, giving you an unbeatable range.

Kick It Up MASTERFUL, COLORFUL, DETAIL-ORIENTED   *Step It Down* SCATTERED, MISCHIEVOUS

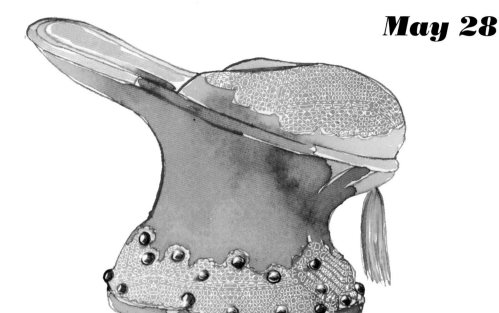

With its silk-cut velvet and its gilt-metal lace trim, this eighteenth-century Italian chopine is as complex and as artfully layered as you. Can you be figured out in one glance? Absolutely not! A true one of a kind, you walk on the unique side of life, creating a formula for success that few can understand. You are fascinating to behold as you dazzle people with your subtle magic. Worn by Venetian courtesans and patricians alike, this original platform shoe allowed the wearer to tower over others in her midst. With your endless quest to climb to new heights, soaring at such high elevations is something you are quite familiar with.

Kick It Up INTRICATE, DAZZLING, INNOVATIVE   *Step It Down* COMPLICATED, HAUGHTY

May 29

Sign ★ GEMINI

As a passionate soul, you're no stranger to the heartfelt energy of the crimson hue of this shoe. You're an empath who can quite literally feel the vibes of the collective consciousness the moment you step into a room. It takes you seconds to size up the scene and accurately assess what's going on. Like this wedge-heeled loafer, you can be at once tempestuous and businesslike. You can easily play the role of the take-charge peacemaker, but it's also easy for you to get sucked into the drama if you don't stay on your toes. It's important for you to think before you speak—your words are a powerful sword that cuts two ways.

Kick It Up PASSIONATE, RADIANT, EMPATHETIC   **Step It Down** DRAMATIC, HARSH

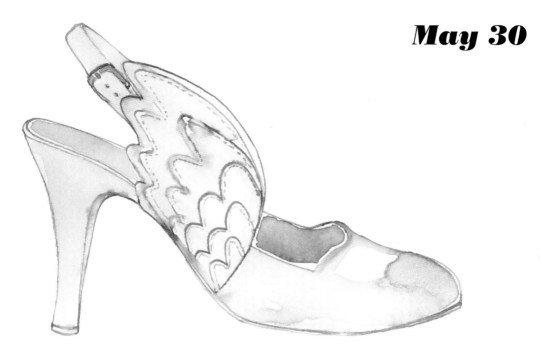

Like this winged vintage slingback, you seem ready to take flight at a moment's notice. A contradiction unto yourself, you manage to keep your head in the clouds and your feet on the Earth at the same time: no easy stunt to pull off. That said, you prefer to float through the ether without too many attachments. Change is often the only constant in your life, and that is purely by your own design. It's anyone's guess where your flights of fancy will lead you, but with your angelic smile and bubbly personality, you're sure to make friends wherever you touch down.

Kick It Up FANCIFUL, ETHEREAL, ADAPTABLE   **Step It Down** FLIGHTY, NONCOMMITTAL

May 31

"**I** saw the angel in the marble, and I carved until I set him free," said Michelangelo of his divinely inspired work. Your own genius follows a similar trajectory. Like this Kate Spade "Vail" slingback, you know exactly what to cut away and what to keep. And like the geometric pattern of this shoe, you can be quite precise and technical. Many people consider you tough, since you're the one saying no more often than yes. One thing's for certain: you always get the job done, whether it's a minor undertaking or a project as elaborate as the Sistine Chapel.

Kick It Up DECISIVE, PRECISE, VISIONARY   *Step It Down* EXACTING, RIGID

Gemini May 22–June 21

JUNE

June 22–July 22 **Cancer**

June 1

"**L**ace—the invention of a goddess and the occupation of a queen,**"** said sixteenth-century French sartorialist Vinciolo. Like the exquisite fabric adorning this sculptured Valentino pump, you are both divine and regal. Intrigue swirls around you: just as the layer of ebony lace cloaks the pump underneath, you can be somewhat veiled about your private life. The truth? You're a highly sensitive soul. Without your shield, you feel as nude as the under-shoe. Fortunately, your stunning exterior creates enough distraction to keep people at bay.

Kick It Up EXQUISITE, INTRIGUING, SENSITIVE   *Step It Down* SUPERFICIAL, ENIGMATIC

Oxford shoes derived their name from the eponymous university in the early 1800s. Originally the domain of scholars, this shoe certainly fits for a brainiac like you. Scientific and philosophical, you greet complex challenges with open arms. You'd make a great detective if you weren't such a social creature. Like this elaborately beaded dinner oxford from the year 1900, you belong at a roundtable of great minds, hashing out the answers to the world's dilemmas. The dynamic angle of this shoe appears to be leaping forward of its own accord. Similarly, you like to stay on the cutting edge of thought, always attuned to what the future has to offer.

Kick It Up INTELLIGENT, SOCIAL, FORWARD-LOOKING   *Step It Down* EMOTIONALLY DETACHED, COMPLICATED

June 3

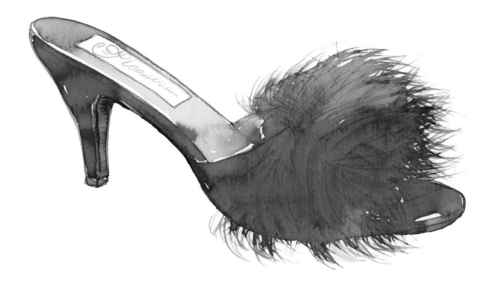

Move over kittens—there's a new vixen in town. This marabou slipper spells "bombshell," and that's exactly what you are. Like an Old Hollywood starlet, you glide through life with an enchanting grace, turning heads and even raising eyebrows. You don't mind a little controversy; in fact, you may even thrive on it. What's the point of living if you can't be a little naughty from time to time? When you're passionate about something, your interest burns red-hot, like the crimson hue of this shoe. Your interests can turn into over-the-top obsessions at times, but hey, you're just not one for half-stepping.

Kick It Up SEDUCTIVE, DARING, PASSIONATE   *Step It Down* OBSESSED, DEFIANT

The road map of your life is not a straight and narrow trajectory. Like this Miu Miu Mary Jane, you are here to collect a patchwork of colorful experiences, which you piece together into a fascinating whole. Part scientist, part detective, you're on an eternal hunt for empirical data. The shoe's unique cutaways echo your passion for slicing beneath the surface and mining for hidden truths. Before you will make a decision or form an opinion, you must examine a situation from every angle. A clever conversationalist, you can be as piercing as the shoe's arrowhead swatches, penetrating people's consciousness with your insight and offbeat ideas.

June 4

Sign ★ GEMINI

June 5

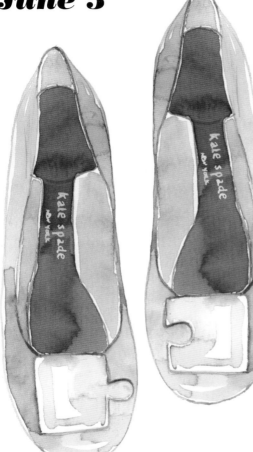

How do the pieces all fit together? Like these Kate Spade "Puzzle" flats, you're fascinated by life's most perplexing enigmas. Bright as the sunshine-yellow hue, you are fundamentally optimistic about your ability to solve any conundrum. You won't stop researching until you've ferreted out the obscure title, the tucked-away tidbit, the ultra-rare reference. You're a bit mercurial, and with your gypsy soul, you've been known to change direction at a moment's notice. The shoe's flat heel is fitting for your meandering style, never slowing you down when you're hot on the heels of some not-so-trivial pursuit.

Kick It Up CLEVER, QUICK, CURIOUS   **Step It Down** INTRUSIVE, FIXATED

Like this flag-inspired Chanel lace-up boot, you are the choicest patriot in town. But you aren't won over easily. Only when a person, place, or passion has captured your heart will you pledge your allegiance for eternity. You love being a supportive partner to the people in your circle. For you, the fun lies in the shared victory. Seeing your friends celebrate personal triumphs fills you with pride. Like the expanse of eyelets dotting this shoe's landscape, you look for openings that allow you to become more entwined with the ones you love. Getting tied up in their lives is not a burden, but something that brings you great joy.

June 6

Sign ★ GEMINI

Kick It Up LOYAL, DISCERNING, SUPPORTIVE   ***Step It Down*** OVERINVOLVED, CLIQUISH

June 7

Step to the side—the queen bee has arrived. A die-hard devotee of fashion, you aren't afraid to use shock value to make a statement. This violet-hued Jeffrey Campbell boot is the perfect accompaniment for your "purple reign." With its platform toe, it elevates you high above your subjects, giving you an added air of authority. The rounded toe is quirky and fun, a nod to your stellar sense of humor. Your ability to laugh at yourself without losing cool points is the amethyst in your crown.

Sign ★ GEMINI

Kick It Up POPULAR, TRENDSETTING, HILARIOUS   ***Step It Down*** DEFIANT, EGOTISTICAL

A **leopard never shows her spots . . . or does she?** In true Gemini fashion, you like to reveal aspects of yourself without ever truly being figured out. The jungle cat markings on this Jimmy Choo sneaker are appropriately muted, a nod to your fierce-yet-enigmatic persona. Never overt, you rely on the element of surprise to work your magic. You prefer to observe from a cool distance before making a swift and sudden pounce; however, at times you can become obsessed with achieving a goal. With a cue from this stylish trainer, pursuing athletic activities will keep you in balance so you don't get carried away while stalking your prey.

Kick It Up STRATEGIC, UNDERSTATED, DEDICATED   *Step It Down* FANATICAL, PREDATORY

June 9

With its fish-eye lens carriage, this quirky "Calder T-strap" from 3.1 Philip Lim seems like an artifact of Alice's Wonderland. Like the fictional heroine, all that's bizarre is beautiful to your eyes. Because you are endlessly inquisitive, your life may become stranger than fiction as you chase after your far-out and fanciful notions. The contrast of the shoe's smooth black leather against the snake-embossed white panel reflects your inner duality. Some days, you feel pulled to just settle down already and find a steady groove. Alas, you can't sit still for long. The lure of your serpentine curiosity always leads you away from those white picket fences and back to the domain of the White Rabbit himself.

Kick It Up WONDROUS, EXPLORATORY, UNEXPECTED　　***Step It Down*** DELUDED, FICKLE

June 10

Like this **Jeffrey Campbell** "Starburst" boot, you light up the night, an incandescent twinkle on an otherwise shadowy landscape. The tiny beadwork reflects your innately hopeful spirit, even though you express your optimism subtly. However, you're not at all afraid of the dark. Exploring the hidden corners of your own psyche is essential to your sense of self-awareness. For you, true bliss cannot be found without experiencing the sharp and aching contrast of melancholy. This boot buckles firmly, keeping the foot snug and protected. Similarly, you require a safe sanctuary to tuck yourself away in, a place to nurse your darkest feelings without interruption or judgment.

Sign ★ GEMINI

Kick It Up HOPEFUL, CHARITABLE, EMPATHETIC   *Step It Down* DEPRESSED, ISOLATED

June 11

Like the cheery blossoms brightening this 1958 Delman cocktail shoe, your can-do spirit is perennial, regenerating itself season after season. Sure, you may have your winters, but you always come back to full bloom when the next inspiring seed is planted in your garden. Whether you're sipping a sidecar or a Manhattan, you love to gather for social occasions. Like this skinny, feminine heel, you know how to be perfectly ladylike when good manners are a must. You also have a bawdy streak, which appears in a timely fashion when people's apathetic attitudes need to be shaken and stirred.

Kick It Up CHEERFUL, OUTGOING, FUN   ***Step It Down*** DISRUPTIVE, LOUD

June 12

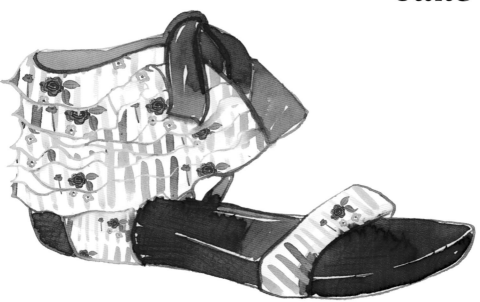

Sugar and spice and everything nice—that's what your sweet soul is made of. Like the ruffled calico print of this Irregular Choice sandal, you remain youthful for eternity. Thank goodness for that! It's your irrepressibly girlish nature that saves you from becoming jaded and cynical. Anne Frank, who shares your birthday, wrote this in her legendary diary while hiding from the Nazis in a cramped attic: "In spite of everything, I still believe that people are really good at heart." Your loving spirit endures through trying times, Valentine red like the sole of this shoe.

Kick It Up FRESH, ENTHUSIASTIC, POSITIVE   *Step It Down* NAIVE, OVERLY TRUSTING

June 13

You're a globe-trotting nomad, so it's anyone's guess what continent you'll be trekking through next. You live not only for the adventure, but for the opportunity to connect and collect, gathering friends from every corner of the Earth. Authenticity ranks high with you, and this moccasin from Osborn Shoes boasts intricate handwoven detailing, straight from the indigenous source. The fabric was fairly made and purchased by this highly ethical brand—ideal since social justice is also a big concern of yours. While your shoes may be dazzling, your aim is to leave the smallest footprint possible so the Earth and all its natural wisdom can remain in balance with the people who inhabit it.

Kick It Up CONSCIOUS, WORLDLY, AUTHENTIC   ***Step It Down*** RIGHTEOUS, NONCOMMITTAL

"Ambition is the path to success," said Renaissance man Bill Bradley. "Persistence is the vehicle you arrive in." Like the former senator/Rhodes scholar/basketball star, you're a go-getter who has her hands in many pots. This quirky Prada wedge is as improbably layered as you. From wood to rubber to jute weave, the shoe's platform brings a mashup of elements as wide-ranging as your talents. Once you've set your sights on a goal, you keep on climbing, rising to formidable heights that would make most people dizzy. Like the menswear detailing on the shoe's carriage, you can be plenty businesslike when needed, often intimidating people without even realizing it.

June 14

Kick It Up MULTIFACETED, HARDWORKING, DETERMINED   ***Step It Down*** INTIMIDATING, RUTHLESS

June 15

A **die-hard romantic,** you live by the code of Romeo and Juliet, willing to give it all up for love. Unlike the Shakespearean couple, however, your engagements are hardly shrouded in secrecy. When your heart is full, you'll shout it from your balcony, wanting the world to share in your rapture. With its dangling leather Valentines and scalloped panels, this "Kiss and Tell" pump from Poetic Licence seduces with an intensity similar to your own. Parting from lovers can leave you as blue as this suede shoe, but you don't stay down for long. You believe in the power of love, and it seems to keep finding you again and again.

Kick It Up ROMANTIC, GENEROUS, WARM   **Step It Down** GULLIBLE, EXHIBITIONISTIC

June 16

Just as leaves on trees burst forth year after year, you are always attuned to life's spring awakenings. You believe in an abundant universe and are capable of flourishing in the scarcest of times. Your optimism, like these Manolo Blahnik boots, remains evergreen. With good reason: the seeds you sow always flourish into a remarkable harvest. Like the decorative tassels on these boots, you enjoy a little pomp and circumstance, but you always keep your feet on the ground. You're excellent at working with "the green," and might find a career in the world of financial planning or money management.

Sign ★ GEMINI

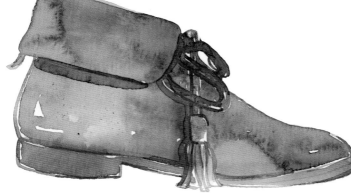

Kick It Up ABUNDANT, OPTIMISTIC, CREATIVE   *Step It Down* AVARICIOUS, OVERZEALOUS

June 17

Sign ★ GEMINI

Every step you take is a bit like a walk of fame. Radiant, mystical, and captivating, you ooze star power from every pore. With its crystal-encrusted detail, this bejeweled Jimmy Choo "Kershaw" mesh pump sparkles with a similar force. You are layered and complex, but like this pump, the pieces come together in an incredibly sexy way. Black is the color of the invisible, and just as dark matter makes up more than 80 percent of our universe, you can be a mystery unto yourself. Even you have no idea where your outsized talents come from. They simply flow through you as if you were a vessel for divine inspiration.

Kick It Up CAPTIVATING, MYSTICAL, GLAMOROUS   *Step It Down* ENIGMATIC, FOREBODING

Like these chic Chanel chain bow flats, you are seen as a respectable individual who has a great head on her shoulders. It's true. A keen decision maker, you are able to boil things down to their black-and-white essence. This is never done without a good deal of thought and investigation. You believe in following due process and can be quite relentless about collecting data and finding clues. The rounded toe and feminine bow soften any severity of this officious pump. Similarly, you know how to sweet-talk people until they drop their guard and give you the answers you are seeking.

Kick It Up KEEN, THOUGHTFUL, RESOLUTE   *Step It Down* MANIPULATIVE, PRYING

June 19

Ladies, start your engines.
You were born with your key in life's ignition, ready to zip off on a daring and rebellious adventure. Like this Dior biker boot, you have a tough-girl edge that is undeniably racy. The alligator is the symbol of survival and adaptability, and the embossed pattern of this biker takes inspiration from this ancient reptile. You too are a survivor, and while you may weather many challenges in this lifetime, they only serve to make you stronger.

Sign ★ GEMINI

Kick It Up ACTIVE, VERSATILE, RESILIENT   ***Step It Down*** RECKLESS, MERCURIAL

A **keen judge of character,** you have the ability to view situations from a multitude of angles. You're not looking for one single answer. Rather, you seek a way to blend contrasting elements into a breathtaking whole. The kaleidoscopic print on this Balenciaga bootie is as colorful as your vision. While you are a linear thinker, you are usually juggling multiple lines of thought at once. That's a lot to handle! Just as these shoes can overstimulate the optic nerve, your ideas may take people on a wild and unpredictable ride. Your moods can be as vivid as these brilliant blue stripes. When you're in a happy place, you are the most motivating cheerleader around!

Sign ★ GEMINI

Kick It Up VISIONARY, EDGY, MOTIVATING ***Step It Down*** PUZZLING, EXHAUSTING

June 21

From opera houses to fine ateliers to the quarters of courtiers, Italian silk brocade has been the chosen fabric of the country's upper class. Similarly, luxury seems to find its way to your doorstep. These 1914 Italian brocade mules share your sumptuous sparkle. Whether you are seated at the table with society's elite or creating luxuriating experiences for others, you understand the toe-curling ecstasy that life's finer things can bring. You're by no means spoiled, however. You work hard for your money, and the green-and-gold hue of this shoe is a nod to your abundant spirit.

Kick It Up LUXURIOUS, GENEROUS, HARDWORKING   *Step It Down* OSTENTATIOUS, OVERINDULGENT

"**L**ove is the wisdom of the fool and the folly of the wise," wrote the eighteenth-century English author Samuel Johnson. A hopeless romantic and intuitive empath, your amorous spirit is the compass that guides your actions. You happily wear your heart on your sleeve or, in the case of this Marc Jacobs wedge sandal, your soles. Like the blush-pink hue of the straps, every ardent encounter feels like the first. You are simply incapable of remaining cynical when your passion takes hold. Your emotional life will be a storied one, the stuff that great movies are made of. Learning to master the wisdom of your heart will be a fascinating lifelong journey.

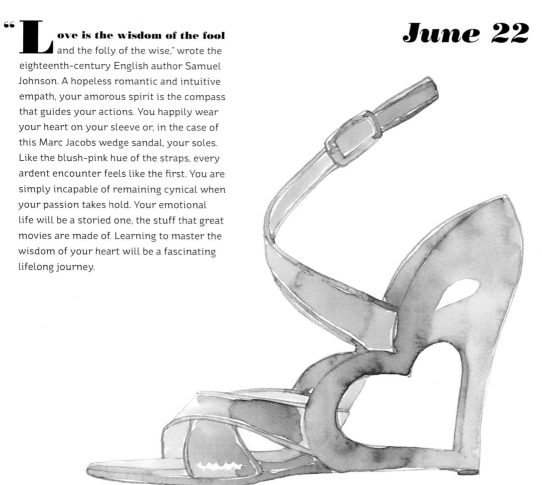

Sign ★ CANCER

June 23

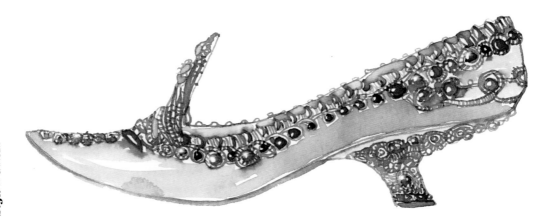

Like the elaborate beadwork on this 1960 Christian Dior kitten heel, you sparkle with a pixie's glow, lighting up the room with your enchanting spirit. The early sixties were a time of irrepressible excess and decadence. You carry a similar wisdom, understanding the power of pleasure to lift the human spirit. You're captivated by the arts and need to surround yourself with beauty at all times. Similar to the nymphlike shape of the shoe, you refuse to let go of your belief in magic. Why should you? You're destined to create a fairy-tale life for yourself, and you'll generously share the spoils of your "happily ever after" with the ones you love.

Kick It Up ENCHANTING, YOUTHFUL, ARTISTIC   ***Step It Down*** MISGUIDED, NAIVE

June 24

The Lucite heel of this Marc Jacobs boot glows a bright and luminescent shade of pink. Similarly, you prefer to view the world through rose-colored glasses, always looking for the positive in any given situation. You're hardly naive, though. Like the businesslike front of this boot, you deal masterfully in the practical realm too. It's your ability to distill logic and magic that makes you so heavenly to be around. With your supportive and caring spirit, you love to help people discover their dreams and develop plans to actualize them. You can make sense from far-out ideas and thrill at the challenge to produce something that people insist cannot be done.

Sign ★ CANCER

Kick It Up POSITIVE, SUPPORTIVE, IMAGINATIVE   ***Step It Down*** NOSY, STUBBORN

June 25

Sign ★ CANCER

With your nurturing nature, you've always got the proverbial kettle on the stove. At a moment's notice, you're there for your loved ones, ready to offer comfort, compassion, and uplifting advice. Like you, this Miu Miu "Teacup" Mary Jane pump brews up a warm and inviting cup. The sheen of its scarlet patent leather burns as brightly as your hearth, which is home to an ever-expanding circle of friends and family. The quirky gold handle flourishing the heel echoes your own imaginative nature. Creativity is your touchstone as you measure the world through the eyes of a true artiste.

Kick It Up WARM, HELPFUL, INVENTIVE   *Step It Down* OVERINVOLVED, MOODY

June 26

A **true water sign,** you are nautical by nature, and the sea is where your passion lies. This classic boat shoe—in navy blue, naturally—keeps you stable when life's waves begin to swell. With your steadfast personality, you're often the one who retains her balance when others are struggling to find their sea legs. As such, you're a trusty captain for your loved ones, the person they count on to steer the ship to safety. Active and outdoorsy, you are impressively energetic. Channeling this energy into an athletic activity helps you to release the emotional stress you unknowingly absorb from helping other people.

Sign ★ CANCER

Kick It Up STEADFAST, ENERGETIC, SUPPORTIVE   **Step It Down** WEIGHTY, LONELY

June 27

The scalloped finish of this 1960s heel takes its inspiration from the gorgeous detailing of seashells. A delicate creature yourself, you often hide behind a pretty shield, safe from the harsher realities of the world. Your sensitivity can feel like a blessing and, at times, a curse. Highly empathetic, you may become swept up in other people's emotions, losing your center in the process. Like the muted brown-and-black tones of this shoe, you prefer to fly under the radar, allowing your work to speak for you. Left to your own devices, it's only a matter of time before you cultivate a stunning and precious pearl.

Kick It Up SWEET, EMPATHETIC, IMAGINATIVE   *Step It Down* UNDERSTATED, DEFENSIVE

June 28

Relics of 1968, this funky Italian leather sandal was created in an era of social change and loud, proud passion for a cause. Fittingly, you can be quite the vocal one when your fiercely protective nature is provoked. You care deeply for people, animals, and all the world's creatures. If you sense mistreatment, look out! Like the complementary-hued orange-and-blue straps of this sandal, you're not afraid to clash in the name of making a statement. You have a heightened understanding of human emotions. Like the reflective heel of this vintage shoe, you can expertly hold up the mirror for people, helping them see themselves as they truly are.

Sign ★ CANCER

Kick It Up PROTECTIVE, PASSIONATE, UNDERSTANDING   **Step It Down** COMBATIVE, HYPERSENSITIVE

June 29

Sign ★ CANCER

With its pastel polka dots, this "Apple Pie" Mary Jane from Poetic Licence is as light, bubbly, and uplifting as you are. You can be an unshakable optimist, buoying people up with your faith alone. "Even if I knew that tomorrow the world would go to pieces, I would still plant my apple tree," wrote sixteenth-century theologian Martin Luther. Like the sweet fruit emblem buttoning this shoe, you are forever sowing the seeds of hope through the universe. Sharing your bumper crop is what makes you happiest of all. You are the bright nucleus of your social circle, the one that people gravitate toward for support and sustenance.

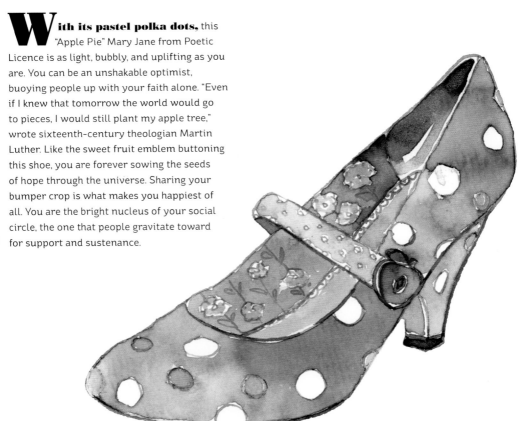

Kick It Up BUOYANT, ENCOURAGING, PRODUCTIVE   **Step It Down** FLIGHTY, SIMPLISTIC

Like this 1993 Manolo Blahnik pump, you read rather stern on the surface. An introvert, you can be pointed with your remarks and laced up rather tightly upon first meeting people. Those who have vision to see beyond the ruse of gray wool and ebony leather are in for a treat. You're hardly a schoolmarm at heart, but rather a sensitive and emotionally adept individual who cares deeply for the world. Security is essential to your sense of harmony, and you'll work hard to build a stable home and put money in the bank. As you learn to be kinder to yourself, you'll find greater compassion for others.

Kick It Up HARDWORKING, STABLE, SENSITIVE   *Step It Down* PRICKLY, FORMAL

June 22–July 22 **Cancer**

JULY

July 23–August 23 **Leo**

"**I**s it a weakness that I lead from my heart, and not my head?" asked Princess Diana, born today. Given that these "Love" flats were designed in her memory by Christian Louboutin, the answer is clearly no. Like the caring, compassionate royal icon, your emotions are your guide. You brighten a room with your warmth, reawakening a sense of hope in all those who you touch. It's only when these flats are side by side that one can read the word love, which is encoded in these shoes. This speaks to you, as partnerships are a central theme in your life. You're a master ambassador and peacemaker who loves being half of a dynamic duo.

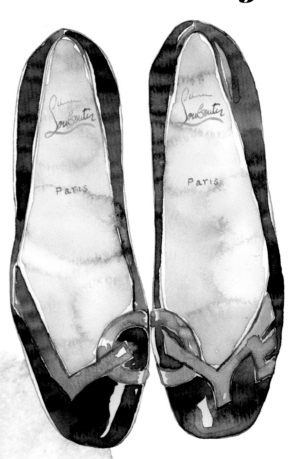

Sign ★ CANCER

Kick It Up ADORING, WARM, COOPERATIVE   *Step It Down* GULLIBLE, HYPERSENSITIVE

July 2

Sign ★ CANCER

The line between fantasy and reality blurs beguilingly in Alexander McQueen's iconic "Armadillo" shoe. That's just the way you like it. With your rich imagination and desire to explore life's mysterious undercurrents, you are drawn to the beautiful and unusual. Like the shoe's breathtakingly high ten-inch stiletto heel, you aren't afraid to take risks, even those that some might consider extreme. The print of this shoe takes its inspiration from a butterfly wing. Metamorphosis is a big theme in your life, as you are forever changing your look. Indeed having a cocoon to retreat to is important for you, but when you're ready to spread your brilliant wings, you make a dazzling impression on the world.

Kick It Up FANCIFUL, DARING, ADAPTABLE   **Step It Down** RECKLESS, ESCAPIST

This lavish 1996 Sciafo mule from Manolo Blahnik mirrors your elegant decadence. An appreciator of fine craftsmanship, you adore bespoke details and know how to create an atmosphere of beauty. A stellar host, your parties are legendary. Like you, the twinkling silver beads and Austrian crystals light up the room. The strand of pearls is a nod to your cool refinement—no one needs to remind you which fork to use. You're the picture of grace and good manners. Like the sixteenth-century slippers Blahnik was inspired by, history is important to you, and you comfortably step into the role of the family matriarch and keeper of traditions.

Kick It Up REFINED, LAVISH, MATRIARCHAL   *Step It Down* MATERIALISTIC, CONTROLLING

July 4

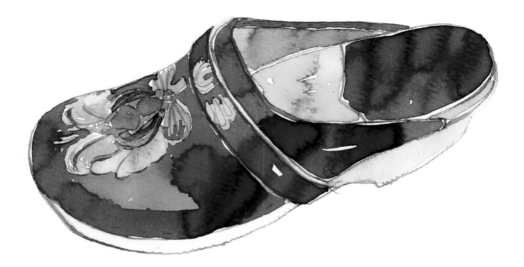

A **born leader and a team player,** you pledge your undying allegiance to any group you're affiliated with. That said, you're far too unique to be an overzealous "joiner" type. Like this flamboyant red Dutch *klompen*, you fit into very specific niches. You adore optimists and people who aren't afraid to color outside the lines of convention. You are highly protective of the ones you love, and keeping your people secure is a big concern. Good thing this clog has been deemed safer than a steel-toed shoe! With its ability to withstand penetration of sharp objects and the splash of dangerous chemicals, this shoe is as industrious as it is vivacious, just like you.

Kick It Up LOYAL, UNCONVENTIONAL, PROTECTIVE   ***Step It Down*** CLIQUISH, IMPENETRABLE

"**The noblest art** is that of making others happy," said circus magnate P. T. Barnum, born today. A spirited caretaker who never loses her sense of childlike wonder, you couldn't agree more. You're here to put a smile on people's faces, touching people on an emotional level as you simultaneously inspire awe. With its flounce of turquoise feathers, this purple "Marlene" sandal by Jimmy Choo transports you to the magical world that lives under the big top. Balancing on this tall stiletto heel might be a bit of a tightrope act, but you happen to enjoy anything that requires a measure of risk. There's never a dull moment when you're in town!

Sign ★ CANCER

Kick It Up AWE-INSPIRING, MAGICAL, UPBEAT   ***Step It Down*** ELUSIVE, DEMANDING

July 6

Women legendarily waited two years for a pair of this in-demand evening shoe created in a 1920s Parisian atelier. With your sophisticated standards and love of life's finer things, you understand the merit of delayed gratification. You're willing to hold out for the best, even if it takes years to manifest. The antique lace veils the body of this shoe, just as you can sometimes be a hard one to read. You're more shy than mysterious, a sensitive soul who will only open up once you are certain you have met someone whom you can trust implicitly. With your dear and intimate circle of friends, you're sure to have a richly rewarding social life.

Kick It Up SOPHISTICATED, PATIENT, INTIMATE   *Step It Down* SUSPICIOUS, CLOSED OFF

July 7

This **"Dance All Night"** platform pump from Poetic Licence belongs on the foot of a nocturnal creature like you. Enigmatic, intriguing, and definitely dreamy, you feel most at home under the glow of ambient lighting. Music touches you at a soul level, and you'd happily spin under the disco ball until the sun peeks above the horizon. Like the shoe's black leather and muted metallic ruche details, you have a fascination with life's shadows and hidden creases. An explorer and a detective, you love the thrill of unraveling a mystery, especially if the hunt for clues leads you to the secret corners of the universe.

Sign ★ CANCER

Kick It Up INTRIGUING, INQUISITIVE, EXPLORATORY   ***Step It Down*** SNEAKY, REBELLIOUS

July 8

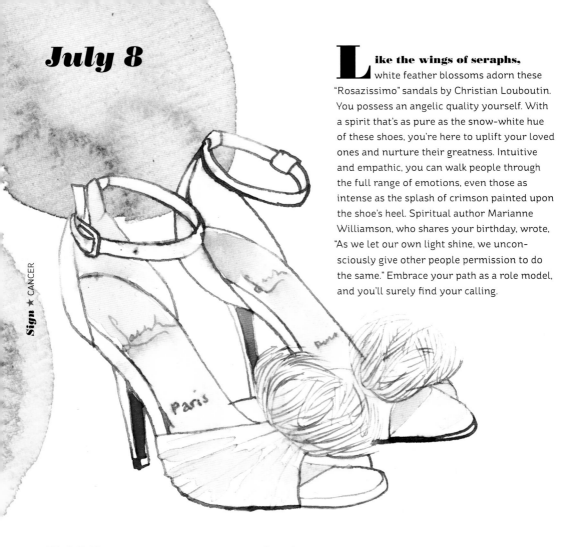

Like the wings of seraphs, white feather blossoms adorn these "Rosazissimo" sandals by Christian Louboutin. You possess an angelic quality yourself. With a spirit that's as pure as the snow-white hue of these shoes, you're here to uplift your loved ones and nurture their greatness. Intuitive and empathic, you can walk people through the full range of emotions, even those as intense as the splash of crimson painted upon the shoe's heel. Spiritual author Marianne Williamson, who shares your birthday, wrote, "As we let our own light shine, we unconsciously give other people permission to do the same." Embrace your path as a role model, and you'll surely find your calling.

Kick It Up EMPATHETIC, UPLIFTING, GUIDING   ***Step It Down*** CODEPENDENT, MOROSE

Tiny birds adorn this Miu Miu "Sparrow" pump, an emblem that does you symbolic justice indeed. Like the small feathered creature, you are forever tending to your nest, foraging for resources, and making sure that your family is warm and safe. You're also a master of camouflage who sometimes prefers to fade into the background so you can keenly observe people from your perch. Like the shoe's white-on-navy print, you also like to create a dramatic effect. The whimsical rounded toe and girlish Mary Jane style reveal your wicked sense of humor and sometimes-mischievous nature.

July 9

Sign ★ CANCER

Kick It Up RESOURCEFUL, PROTECTIVE, HUMOROUS   **Step It Down** GUARDED, TROUBLEMAKING

July 10

Like this deconstructed **"Ines" oxford from Alexander Wang,** you like to pick things apart so you can reveal and understand their inner workings. Endlessly curious, you won't stop digging until you find the answers you seek. You're highly sensitive and allow only a chosen few to step into your inner circle. With its protruding heel, this shoe gives a classic oxford an unusual spin. Similarly, you know how to use subtle visual cues to make a strong point. Your own edgy fashion sense has been known to stir up intrigue, helping you break the ice with people who are drawn to your sense of style.

Kick It Up PATIENT, EMPATHETIC, OBSERVANT   ***Step It Down*** CRITICAL, ISOLATED

July 11

Peekaboo! The fanlike throat of this Seychelles "Mamie" bootie reveals and conceals simultaneously. You're no stranger to games of hide-and-seek. Part of you longs to be admired and adored, and like the scalloped lace cutouts in the leather, you bring a powerfully feminine flourish to all that you do. You have your shy and sensitive side too and can be as delicate as the seashell-pink tone of this shoe. Retreating to a private hideaway is essential to your sense of balance. While you love to travel, it's equally important that you can return to a solid home base.

Sign ★ CANCER

Kick It Up TANTALIZING, DELICATE, ADORABLE ***Step It Down*** CONFUSING, UNREACHABLE

July 12

Like these Prada wedges, you are classic cool with a spunky twist. The two-tone nude-and-black leather appeals to your ladylike charm. A natural matriarch, you're well aware of the Miss Manners playbook, and you're willing to follow convention when the situation calls for it. Your preference, however, is to bend those rules. The oversize silver buckle on the toe and the quirky cutout heel are not Emily Post's terrain. Your creativity is your calling card, and people rely on you to help them think outside the box without losing touch with reality. You're an unwavering supporter, but let people give back to you too!

Kick It Up WELL-MANNERED, CREATIVE, MATRIARCHAL   **Step It Down** OVEREXTENDED, SLY

Just as water becomes ice, you are a master of transformation. When it's time to change, you boldly shape-shift into your next incarnation. This "Skate" shoe by Jeffrey Campbell is emblematic of your ability to glide gracefully into new opportunities. With its intricate cutaway heel and quirky peep-toe, this is the shoe of a daring free-thinker. While you're undeniably cool, you're never a frosty ice queen. Sure, you might intimidate people with your triple Axel jumps, but with your nurturing nature, most folks warm to you the instant you say hello.

Sign ★ CANCER

Kick It Up GRACEFUL, DRIVEN, NURTURING   ***Step It Down*** OPPORTUNISTIC, SCATTERED

July 14

With its seductive cheetah print, this Kate Spade "Trini" ankle boot is definitely fierce. You're quite the head turner yourself, fearlessly exhibiting your spots and wearing your heart on your sleeve. Of all the jungle cats, the cheetah has the greatest potential for being domesticated. While you live an exciting life in the public eye, you can be a hard-core homebody too. With its girlish bow and sleek silhouette, this boot is the walking definition of feminine wiles. While you're an excellent huntress, you rarely have to chase after anything. You simply attract it to you with your tantalizing charms.

Kick It Up FASCINATING, SEDUCTIVE, INTRIGUING **Step It Down** MANIPULATIVE, UNRELIABLE

Calm, capable, and in control, you're an alpha female who rules with a cool head. This Jimmy Choo pump was made for a powerful lady like you. Its embossed crocodile print and pointed toe are all business—even a tad intimidating. You cut an impressive figure yourself. While you're willing to negotiate, smart people know better than to cross you. You can be a formidable enemy when pushed to your limit. With its sexy cutout sides, this shoe doesn't hide much. You may be private, but you have no need for secrecy. You're too confident to play that kind of game, and besides, your hard-won merit speaks for itself.

Kick It Up POWERFUL, CAPABLE, COOL   **Step It Down** INTIMIDATING, AGGRESSIVE

July 16

Sign ★ CANCER

Variety is the spice of your life, and if anything gets too predictable, you'll be the first to shake it up. This 1930s satin ballroom dance shoe is a nod to your ability to gracefully glide from one experience to the next without missing a beat. Like the unassuming diamond buckle, you sparkle without being over the top. Although you make it all seem effortless, you are a hard worker who puts a great deal of thought into her actions. Ginger Rogers, who was born on this day, pulled off the same moves as Fred Astaire—except she danced backward and in heels. No small feat! Like Ginger, seamless grace is the secret ingredient to your pièce de résistance.

Kick It Up EXCITING, GRACEFUL, DRIVEN   *Step It Down* COMPLICATED, SECRETIVE

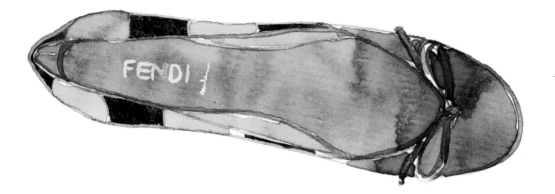

Modest and sweet, you don't believe in fighting for the spotlight. You prefer to take the understated approach, wowing with classic good taste and practical magic. This tri-toned Fendi ballet flat is chic and discriminating, a nod to your stellar judgment and abilities. The striped canvas body creates a fun juxtaposition to the businesslike leather toe, bringing playful levity to the shoe. Using your wry sense of humor, you can always lighten the mood when things get too heavy. However, people should not mistake your kindness for weakness. You're a force to be reckoned with, even if you are making your power plays from behind the scenes.

Kick It Up TASTEFUL, WITTY, SHARP   **Step It Down** ASCETIC, CALCULATING

July 18

Versatile, curious, and exploratory, you are an eager pupil of life. Although you require a secure home life, you seek experiences outside of your comfort zone as well. This navy Stella McCartney buckle flat mirrors your adaptable nature. Sporty and tasteful, it could as easily be worn for a business meeting as for a casual afternoon with the ladies who lunch. The slight platform of the crepe sole gives the shoe a playful edge. You do enjoy the good life, and laughter is your soul's ultimate medicine. Yet when it's time to get serious, you're as polished and as no-nonsense as the loafer's patent leather body.

Kick It Up ADAPTABLE, CURIOUS, POLISHED   **Step It Down** SEVERE, JUDGMENTAL

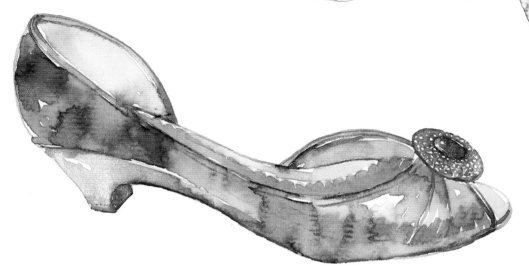

Sign ★ CANCER

Highly adaptable, this "Golden Tea" dance shoe shapes to the foot, fitting itself gracefully along the individual wearer's curves and arches. That's how you flow through life. An empathetic soul with a skilled understanding of human emotions, you are able to shift your energy to suit the needs of the people in your midst. You're excellent in a crisis and stellar in social situations. Although you're highly versatile, you're no chameleon. Like the shoe's brushed-gold leather and jeweled detailing, you emanate glamour and tend to stand out in crowds while simultaneously fitting right in.

Kick It Up EMPATHETIC, FLEXIBLE, GLAMOROUS   *Step It Down* UNGROUNDED, LENIENT

July 20

Like this plucky 1970s Italian leather platform sandal, you're all about raising yourself to new heights—often at an elevation where only thrill seekers dare tread. Like the brown, orange, and yellow strips of leather, you often find yourself woven into some pretty colorful situations. Hey, at least you're never bored! Like the sinuous curves of the shoe's wooden heel, you have a seductively feminine allure. You're definitely dramatic and undeniably fun to watch in action.

Kick It Up THEATRICAL, ENTERTAINING, SEDUCTIVE   ***Step It Down*** MELODRAMATIC, TROUBLE SEEKING

Saucy and in your face, you're an irrepressible mischief maker. You just can't help yourself: you get a little kick out of pushing people's buttons, especially the straight-laced types. This "Bormio Spice" combat boot from Hunter is your perfect armor. With its poppy-saffron hue, it doesn't exactly say, "Let's go to war," and that's a good thing. You're not here to make enemies; you just want people to lighten up. Like the boot's thick, weatherproof rubber, you can be rather self-protective too. Underneath the jokes, you're a sensitive soul. Don't use your humor to deflect people from getting to know the real—and downright amazing—you.

Sign ★ CANCER

Kick It Up MISCHIEVOUS, WITTY, BRAVE   ***Step It Down*** DEFENSIVE, BRASH

July 22

Sign ★ CANCER

This Balenciaga tube slingback sandal is nearly a hybrid of a bootie. Simultaneously concealing and revealing, it echoes your own inner divide. Being born on the cusp of cautious Cancer and attention-loving Leo is not an easy line to walk. Half of you longs to disappear into a private hideaway, as the generous leather tube strap of this shoe suggests. Yet there's an irrepressible performer peeking out, ready to bare her soul for the world. Like the dramatic angle of the shoe's gray leather body, you need peak experiences to draw you out of your shell. With your deep emotional understanding, you can connect to an audience at a powerfully intuitive level.

Kick It Up INSPIRING, EMPATHETIC, ENTERTAINING   **Step It Down** COVERT, MELODRAMATIC

You're the queen of sustainability, skilled at stretching resources and creating things of long-lasting value. Like this Stella McCartney "vegan leather" pump, you know that conservation does not have to go hand in hand with a conservative appearance. The pop of pink brightens up the earthy brown and cream of this pump while the spiky stiletto heel is a nod to your undeniable glamour. With your strong ethical code, you believe in laying all your cards on the table. Similarly, the rose-hued area of the shoe is made from transparent material. Since you have nothing to hide, you have everything to gain. People trust you implicitly and rely on you as their capable leader.

Sign ★ LEO

Kick It Up RESOURCEFUL, GLAMOROUS, TRUSTWORTHY   *Step It Down* FRUGAL, JUDGMENTAL

July 24

This Christian Louboutin "Highness 160" is a limited-edition pump and, like you, is part of an exclusive collection. Hardworking and competitive, you earn your place among the elite. As the embellished "Hollywood" letters insinuate, fame seems to finds its way to your doorstep. Not that you don't chase it a little yourself. Like the stiletto's beads and sequins, you're attracted to the sparkle in life. The bright lights of the big city call you, which is why the shoe's street-style spunk hits the mark with a cosmopolitan diva like yourself.

Kick It Up ADVENTUROUS, EXCITING, MAGNETIC   **Step It Down** UNSTABLE, FLIGHTY

Forget about the gray days.
Like this rainbow wedge sandal from Jimmy Choo, you are a colorful character who always looks on the bright side of life like a walking one-woman show. You keep people spellbound with your bold, lively, and effusive personality. The braided leather straps have an ethnic-inspired feel, and as a traveler and seeker, you're here to soak up wisdom from the farthest corners of the globe. The ancient tradition of oral history speaks to you. You love to hear, share, and tell stories and can spin a fascinating yarn yourself.

Sign ★ LEO

Kick It Up EFFUSIVE, FRIENDLY, WISE   ***Step It Down*** EXAGGERATED, GULLIBLE

July 26

The metal horsebit detail was introduced by Gucci to its loafer design in the early 1950s and has since become an iconic stamp of the brand. Like the silver clasps, you add a signature touch to all that you do. Classic elegance is your personal seal, and like this loafer, you are truly timeless in your appeal. Strong and dependable, you don't mind if people rely on you; in fact, you welcome it. A born leader, you are everyone's favorite wise woman, the one who keeps a cool head in the face of pressure.

Kick It Up CLASSIC, RELIABLE, WISE   *Step It Down* PRAGMATIC, FRUGAL

All hail the queen of the jungle! Like this Donna Karan platform sandal, you bear the markings of a fierce and regal tribeswoman. The gold beaded strap adorns the shoe like a crown; the chunky wooden sole lifts you to the heights of leadership that are so naturally your realm. Earthy tones of cream, tan, and umber echo your talent for working with natural resources. You know how to draw out the best in people and maximize the value of the materials you use. No wonder your relationships have such a high sustainability quotient!

July 27

Kick It Up REGAL, EARTHY, RESOURCEFUL ***Step It Down*** OVERBEARING, CHEAP

July 28

This vintage Ferragamo flat was designed as an homage to Jacqueline Kennedy, who was born today. Like the iconic First Lady, you were meant to rise to a prominent position in this lifetime. Poised, graceful, and ever mindful of your manners, you enjoy the richness of tradition and formalities. That said, you do have a spunky streak, which often takes people by surprise. Like the cheery sunshine-yellow leather of these flats, you always look on the bright side of life. Jackie O once said, "One must not let oneself be overwhelmed by sadness." People can count on you to brighten the mood and mine for the golden opportunity in any situation.

Sign ★ LEO

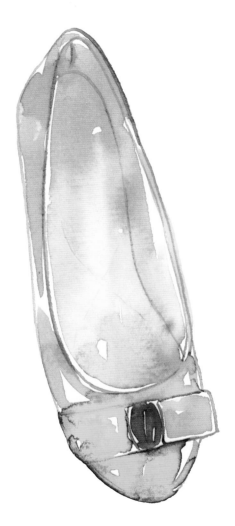

Kick It Up OPTIMISTIC, WELL-MANNERED, SOCIAL ***Step It Down*** SELF-IMPORTANT, STRICT

This Yves St. Laurent pump was designed in 1985, during an earlier era of punk. With its crisscross black patent leather straps and piercing crystal studs on the body and heel, it's edgy and fierce, just like you. You've been known to intimidate a few people in your day. You can't help it: your confidence and unstoppable drive are simply awe inspiring. The punk movement was all about in-your-face self-expression, just as you're known for being a fierce maverick and individual. Like the pump's pointed toe, when you're focused on a mission, you aim right for the target until you get the job done.

Kick It Up EDGY, CONFIDENT, DRIVEN **Step It Down** AGGRESSIVE, INTIMIDATING

July 30

All the world's your stage! Like this wacky 1980s Vivienne Westwood platform, you enjoy making a spectacle of yourself. Theatrical and unconventional, you rise high above the Average Janes. Like its breathtakingly high heel, you're comfortable being hoisted onto a pedestal. Face it, kid: you were born to be a star. There's nothing modest about this shoe's curves, and why should there be? As far as you're concerned, if you've got it, flaunt it—as you definitely will do amid the thundering applause of your ever-growing fan base.

Sign ★ LEO

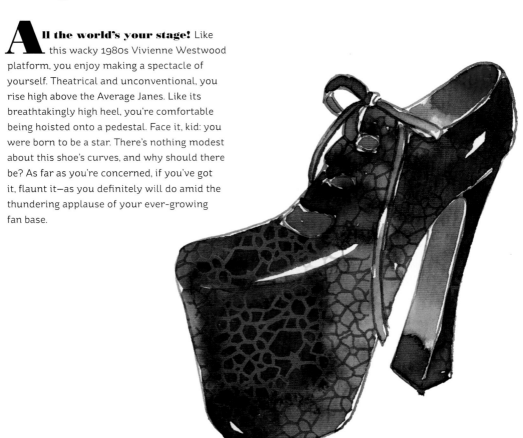

Kick It Up STURDY, SENSUOUS, DECISIVE   **Step It Down** ANXIOUS, REPRESSED

July 31

Creative, kind, and benevolent, you are a "giver" of the most magical variety. Forever dreaming up ways to make the world a better place, your creativity is your compass on this quest. Jimmy Choo's spin on the famed "ruby slippers" was designed for an auction benefitting the Pediatric AIDS Foundation. With its deep-red snakeskin and crystal embellishments, it is "off to see the Wizard," just like your wild imagination so often is. All the more so when a good cause is involved. Nobody can plan a benefit bash, fund-raiser, or party more artfully than you.

Sign ★ LEO

Kick It Up PHILANTHROPIC, THOUGHTFUL, MAGICAL   ***Step It Down*** EXCESSIVE, IRRATIONAL

July 23–August 23 **Leo**

AU·GUST

August 24–September 22 *Virgo*

August 1

Some might call you aggressive, prickly even. You don't mind. You're a woman with a vision who won't stop until she's reached the top. Like this spiky stiletto, you know how to drive your point home, sharply. You're incredibly persuasive, however, and usually wind up getting your way. In personal affairs, you aren't the easiest to get close to. Your studded exterior can keep the meek and mild at bay. That's fine by you. At heart, you're a powerhouse who prefers the company of people who can confidently command any room.

Sign ★ LEO

Kick It Up AMBITIOUS, PERSUASIVE, CONFIDANT ***Step It Down*** AGGRESSIVE, IRRITABLE

August 2

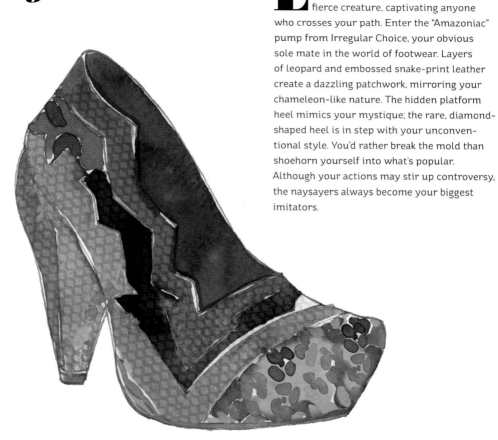

Like a feline fatale, you're one fierce creature, captivating anyone who crosses your path. Enter the "Amazoniac" pump from Irregular Choice, your obvious sole mate in the world of footwear. Layers of leopard and embossed snake-print leather create a dazzling patchwork, mirroring your chameleon-like nature. The hidden platform heel mimics your mystique; the rare, diamond-shaped heel is in step with your unconventional style. You'd rather break the mold than shoehorn yourself into what's popular. Although your actions may stir up controversy, the naysayers always become your biggest imitators.

Kick It Up DAZZLING, UNCONVENTIONAL, FIERCE **Step It Down** MISLEADING, RUTHLESS

"As soon as there is life, there is danger," wrote Ralph Waldo Emerson. Perhaps that explains your early proclivities for living on the edge. You seem to find yourself in the line of fire more often than most. Could it be because you place yourself there? Like a heroic action figure, you're Tank Girl meets Wonder Woman—and these red biker booties from Alexander McQueen are perfectly suited to your kick-ass personality. The skull zipper warns those impending bad guys, "Don't even think about crossing me!" Learning to choose your battles is one of life's great lessons. Before you rush in for the save, make sure people actually *want* to be rescued.

Kick It Up HEROIC, PRINCIPLED, BRAVE **Step It Down** COMBATIVE, ARROGANT

August 4

You're a feisty, fiery trailblazer, which is why this sparkling Gucci heel is your partner-in-shoe. This pump glitters incandescently with each step—perfect for someone known for illuminating opportunities for other people. You're a social butterfly with a flair for the theatrical, and so it's no coincidence that you'd match up with a shoe that is the domain of disco kids and cabaret dancers. You are famous for breaking through the so-called glass ceiling and as such, will have many successors following in your footsteps in this lifetime.

Kick It Up BRIGHT, TRAILBLAZING, THEATRICAL *Step It Down* INCONSIDERATE, BOASTFUL

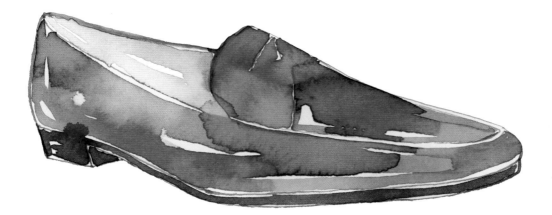

The classic penny loafer is the province of a smart, sensible, and hardworking woman, which aptly describes you. You are always aware of the bottom line and won't move ahead with plans until they are budgeted, mapped out, and finessed to airtight certainty. Like Prada's bright cyan spin on this traditionally understated shoe, you are also quite the colorful character. Your emotional instincts are as sharp as your measured pragmatism, and the more you use them, the better. Allow for some imagination along with the perspiration when tackling those outsize projects.

Kick It Up LEVELHEADED, SHARP, INSTINCTUAL   *Step It Down* CONTROLLING, UNIMAGINATIVE

August 6

Cynics, begone! You're a dreamy idealist who prefers to view life through an ethereal and imaginative lens. Your fairy-tale fantasies come to life in Jeffrey Campbell's "Michelle" shoe, an enchanting spin on the classic pump. Its unicorn heel spirals into a ruffled throat, resembling the bodice of a fairy princess's gown. Many will gallop to your castle door, but few will make it past your drawbridge. You're saving your heart for someone special, and someday that prince is sure to come.

Sign ★ LEO

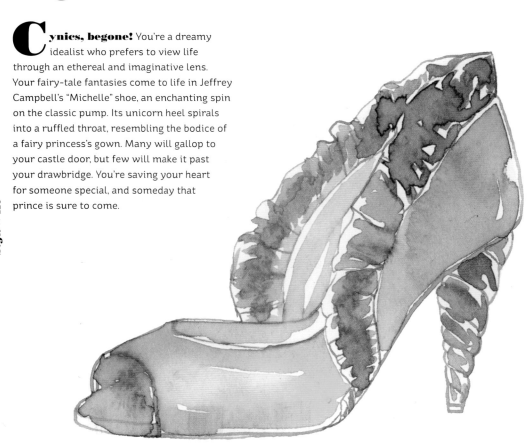

Kick It Up ENCHANTING, OPTIMISTIC, ALLURING   ***Step It Down*** UNREALISTIC, MISGUIDED

Mysterious as a Bond girl, you like to slip in the side door, observing your subjects from a cool distance before cracking the case. Like you, this Louboutin loafer flies under the radar without falling into anonymity. The metal-and-chain detail toe cap is unique but also fairly impenetrable. Similarly, you can be a tough nut to crack. Revealing what's concealed is one of your gifts, and you're great at mining the truth from people. Although it can be scary, learn to uncover more information about yourself. You'll discover a truly fulfilling way to "bond" as you expand your circle of true friends and confidantes.

Kick It Up INTUITIVE, SHARP, INSIGHTFUL   ***Step It Down*** DECEPTIVE, CLOSED OFF

August 8

This **"Quetzal" bootie from Osborn Shoes** shares its name with a brightly plumed tropical bird. You're a flamboyant figure yourself, fluttering around from place to place, absorbing wisdom from each experience. With your many talents and interests, your life will never follow a predictable pattern. You're as versatile as the shoe's recycled folk fabric, yet as dependable as the true-blue denim adorning the toe. Diversity is a key theme in your life. From the countries you visit to the people you befriend, you are truly a global citizen.

Kick It Up CULTURED, EXPLORATORY, TALENTED ***Step It Down*** OVEREXTENDED, UNFOCUSED

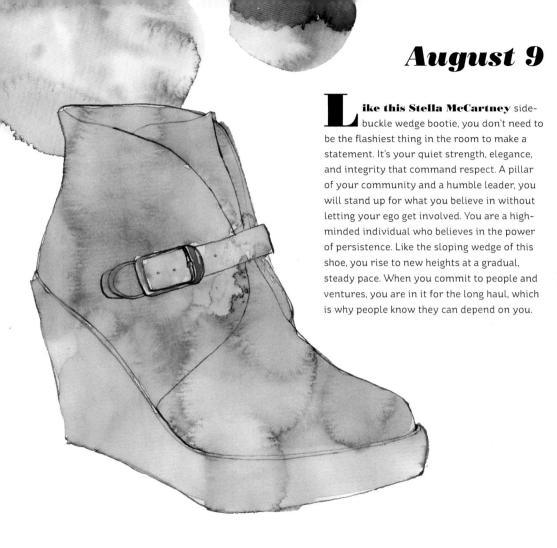

August 9

Like this **Stella McCartney** side-buckle wedge bootie, you don't need to be the flashiest thing in the room to make a statement. It's your quiet strength, elegance, and integrity that command respect. A pillar of your community and a humble leader, you will stand up for what you believe in without letting your ego get involved. You are a high-minded individual who believes in the power of persistence. Like the sloping wedge of this shoe, you rise to new heights at a gradual, steady pace. When you commit to people and ventures, you are in it for the long haul, which is why people know they can depend on you.

Sign ★ LEO

Kick It Up MODEST, DEPENDABLE, LOYAL   *Step It Down* JUDGMENTAL, OVERBURDENED

August 10

It's showtime! Like this Kate Spade "Linette" feathered pump, you announce yourself with a theatrical flounce that is both seductive and playful. You're a born entertainer whose emotions flow as deep as the wine-colored hue of this heel. You're capable of channeling a wide range of emotions, leaving your audience spellbound. The elegant plumage on the toe says "silver screen starlet," while the cheeky bow echoes your girlish charm. While your public image is vivid, your private persona can be vague. That's because you so easily go in and out of character, so be mindful that you don't disappear in the process.

Kick It Up THEATRICAL, SPELLBINDING, EMPATHETIC **Step It Down** ALL-CONSUMED, OSTENTATIOUS

August 11

It's been said that the mirror has two faces: one that reflects what we want to see, another that casts back the shadows we'd rather ignore. You are a lot like that looking glass, helping people glimpse the full picture of themselves with your honest appraisal. Like the mirrored shell of this shoe, the "truth" all depends on the angle you're viewing life through. Be compassionate, and remember that perception is reality. Fortunately, you have an ability to see many sides of a situation, which makes you an amazingly enlightened individual.

Sign ★ LEO

Kick It Up HONEST, PERCEPTIVE, ENLIGHTENED   *Step It Down* HARSH, CRITICAL

August 12

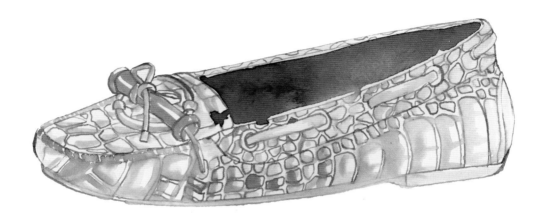

Like this preppy Dior loafer, you are a traditionalist at heart. You find comfort in time-tested wisdom and practices, taking it upon yourself to keep them alive. As feminine as the muted pink hue, you glide easily into the role of the matriarch, gathering people together to uphold family or community rituals. At times, you can be a bit hard nosed, like the shoe's square toe. The tied cord and nautical-style grommets and lacing are emblematic of your love of all things classic. The loafer's crocodile embossing reflects your powerful ability to remain sturdy and timeless, keeping ideas alive decade after decade through your sheer resilience.

Kick It Up WISE, ELEGANT, GENERATIVE   *Step It Down* OLD-FASHIONED, FIXED

August 13

Luck be a lady! You have an uncanny knack for coming out the winner, even when the odds seem stacked against you. These fringed cowgirl boots could have been worn by legendary female sharpshooter Annie Oakley, who shares your birthday. Like her, you're known for hitting targets that few can reach, much less spy altogether. It's easy for people to underestimate you at first, since you don't like being the flashiest person in the room. You'd rather show than tell, but once you break out your show-stopping talents, all eyes are on you!

Sign ★ LEO

Kick It Up FORTUITOUS, OUTSPOKEN, RESILIENT   ***Step It Down*** ABRASIVE, SELF-CENTERED

August 14

For a smarty-pants like you, it's all too obvious that geek can be chic. Your insightful viewpoints always come along with a dash of tongue-in-cheek humor. With its raised heel and gingham trim, this "Backlash" bootie from Poetic Licence speaks your language, infusing mischievous spice into its schoolgirl charm. The clever contrast of the laces echoes your ability to pull together unexpected elements, inspiring people to think outside of the box. The sunshine yellow scores high marks for brightness, perfect for an A student like you.

Kick It Up INTELLECTUAL, WITTY, MISCHIEVOUS   *Step It Down* SUPERIOR, OVERANALYTICAL

"**S**ensuality without love is a sin; love without sensuality is worse than a sin," wrote Spanish poet José Bergamin. As someone who loves to touch, taste, feel, and experience life to its fullest, you know these words to be true. Goddesslike, you are magnetic and powerful, and people bow to you like refined royalty. This "Resin Leaves" sandal by Alexander McQueen is befitting of your glamorous and earthy charms. Gold is your color: you are also quite the alchemist, known for turning that which has been trashed into indisputable treasure.

Sign ★ LEO

Kick It Up MAGNETIC, REFINED, GODDESSLIKE   ***Step It Down*** UNTOUCHABLE, HEDONISTIC

August 16

Like the high-voltage, zigzag pattern on this high-top sneaker, you are forever on the move. Your path is hardly a straight-and-narrow one. A nonconformist to the core, you defy convention at every turn; some might even call you a rebel. That's fine by you. Expressing your individuality, with an exaggerated flair, is what makes your heart sing. Although you enjoy standing out of the crowd, you're a true "people person." You have friends from all walks of life and every corner of the globe—and like a cultural ambassador, you love bringing them all together.

Kick It Up ENERGETIC, NONCONFORMIST, FRIENDLY   *Step It Down* RECKLESS, DEFIANT

"Let's get straight down to business" is the air you project when you walk into a room. You're not big on ostentatious displays of status, but you still manage to carry yourself with a commanding, even regal air. This Marc Jacobs lace-up shares your authoritative nature, the stacked heel rising high like your ambitions. With its high-polished sheen and finely detailed gold hardware, it speaks to your standard of excellence. You want everything done to the letter, and you don't suffer fools lightly. At times you can be intimidating, but ultimately, people respect you for your commitment to creating works of quality and distinction.

Kick It Up INFLUENTIAL, REGAL, SELECTIVE   ***Step It Down*** NITPICKY, INTIMIDATING

August 18

Sign ★ LEO

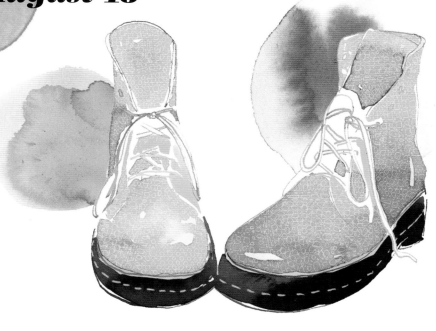

Like these sunshine-yellow stompers, your disposition is both cheery and authoritative at once. Their brilliant gold color is the perfect metaphor for your rich creativity and radiant personality. You emanate brightness, heat, and an enduring strength that people circle around for warmth. Standing out from the crowd is your preference; you hate to be lumped in with others unless you're leading the charge of a team effort. For certain, fun time ranks high on your list of must-haves, but you also bring a weighty work ethic to the table. The truth? You're bored by anything that comes too easily to you. That's why you tackle each challenge with a can-do spirit.

Kick It Up PASSION, WARMTH, DRIVE   ***Step It Down*** BOSSINESS, STUBBORNNESS

August 19

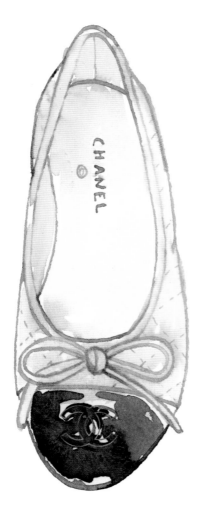

"**A girl should be two things:** classy and fabulous," pronounced couture legend Coco Chanel, who shares your birthday. Like the fashion designer, you are true It Girl material. Her eponymous ballet flat is luxurious while keeping you light on your feet. You are too fascinated by life's discoveries to be slowed down by a high-maintenance heel. Like Chanel herself, you are a trendsetter and a magnet for all things fabulous—oh, the people you'll rub elbows with in this lifetime! Pride can be your Achilles' heel, however, so be careful not to get too caught up in appearances, or it can be lonely at the top.

Sign ★ LEO

Kick It Up CAPTIVATING, TRENDSETTING, LUXURIOUS   *Step It Down* SUPERFICIAL, PROUD

August 20

Shimmering and opalescent, this Jimmy Choo bootie stirs up desire and imagination with each step. You are much the same: a dream weaver who might use these very gleaming threads to spin a rich fantasy. If you had your way, you'd be on a permanent vacation from the harsher realities of life. You're prone to escapism, but it's that very ability to travel beyond the realms of the tangible that is your greatest gift. You enchant with your creativity and may use art, music, décor, and other sensory tools to architect alternate worlds that people can step into.

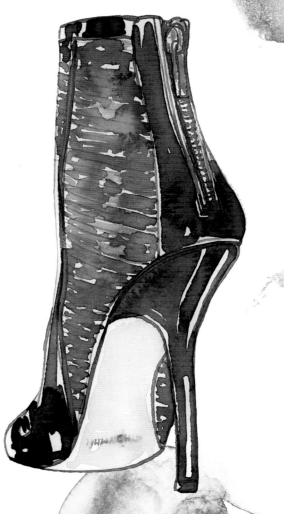

Kick It Up IMAGINATIVE, FLUID, GENIUS   *Step It Down* ESCAPIST, DISCONNECTED

You have a subtle-yet-delicious way of captivating people's attention.
Using the power of the paradox, you simplify, downplay, and even fly under the radar, but not for long. Being the proverbial black swan in a flock filled with ivory always turns heads in your directions. Discreet as you may appear on the surface, there's always a surprise inside. This understated black loafer might not scream "wild child" at first blush, but the geometric lining reveals another story. Your inner life is rich and colorful, a lucky discovery for those who tread beyond your surface appearance.

Kick It Up DISCREET, SURPRISING, DEEP   *Step It Down* SECRETIVE, PERPLEXING

August 22

No-nonsense pragmatism collides with sporty chic in Hunter's spin on the classic Wellington. You're as industrious as they come, just like this hardy, resilient boot. Rough-and-tumble situations don't intimidate you; in fact, you're often the first one to jump into the fray. Like the poreless rubber of these "Wellies," your tough-girl veneer can seem impenetrable, but you have an equally playful side. Your ability to laugh at yourself and the absurdity of the world around you makes you highly accessible—not to mention fun to be around. Charitable and bighearted, helping other people brings you great joy. At times, you're so generous you could practically walk on water.

Kick It Up RESILIENT, INDUSTRIOUS, GENEROUS *Step It Down* AGGRESSIVE, IMPENETRABLE

Like the gilded toe cap of this Christian Louboutin power pump, your internal compass points straight toward the gold standard. You want the best in everything, and you're willing to work hard for it. Accomplished, striking, and graceful, you glide past life's red velvet ropes, straight for the VIP suite. You are precise and technical, capable of cool detachment when the situation calls for it. Since the time of ancient Egyptians, crimson soles have been the mark of wealth and social status. Being a magnet for life's finer things yourself, it's only fitting that you kick up your feet among the well-heeled members of society.

August 23

Sign ★ LEO

Kick It Up GRACEFUL, DETERMINED, SUCCESSFUL *Step It Down* REMOVED, COLD

August 24

Sign ★ VIRGO

Move over, Nancy Drew. With this "Wordsearch" patterned high-top from Converse, no one has to tell you to get a clue. You're already on the case, scouting out rare finds, cool-hunting for obscure trends, researching new hotspots, and emerging the preeminent know-it-all in the pack. For you, life is a never-ending puzzle to be solved, and you have an eye for discovering hidden delights. Anything too simple or too obvious just bores you! A born wordsmith, you are adept with language and may choose a career that involves writing, speaking, or linguistics.

Kick It Up CLEVER, INTELLIGENT, COOL   *Step It Down* DETACHED, OVERANALYTICAL

August 25

You're an earthy sensualist who prefers the most full-bodied experiences that life has to offer. Tactile encounters turn you on: you enjoy physical contact and may be quite a nimble athlete. Like this red fetishwear sandal, you may find yourself dancing on the edgier side of life, getting lost in the rapture of the moment. You're equal parts impish and innocent, and should you realize that you've crossed the line of propriety, your cheeks may blush as brightly as the crimson hue of this shoe. Nevertheless, you'll be the first to admit that you're not *that* innocent.

Sign ★ VIRGO

Kick It Up AGILE, SENSUAL, RAPTUROUS ***Step It Down*** HEDONISTIC, UNREALISTIC

August 26

Generous and helpful, you love being of service to people, especially when you are all working toward the higher good of humanity. This modest boat shoe from Hunter echoes your sensible, low-key vibe. You'd rather be first mate than captain, since organizing people is more your passion than steering the ship. An equally weighted cargo is the one that will stay afloat the longest. Make sure to crew up with people who are as supportive as you are, so you don't wind up shouldering more than your share of the load.

Kick It Up EMPATHETIC, DETAIL-ORIENTED, LOVING   *Step It Down* SELF-SACRIFICING, REPRESSED

"**We shall never know** all the good that a simple smile can do," encouraged Mother Teresa, who was born on this day. Like the saintly nun's, your charitable spirit knows no bounds. Bringing light to the suffering is one of your life's missions, whether you're beaming bright energy in passing or getting down in the trenches for a cause you believe in. A modest style worn by another social activist, these leather sandals that Gandhi once wore keep you in stride with the issues of the everyday man. Like both legendary leaders, you believe that peaceful revolutions are the one true way to bring about change.

Sign ★ VIRGO

Kick It Up HUMBLE, GENEROUS, ELEVATED   **Step It Down** OVEREXTENDED, WOEFUL

August 28

Bring on the turns of phrase and extended metaphors. You have a way with words and love nothing more than a rich conversational exchange. From glib rep-artee to probing intellectual dialogues, you'll keep a solid foothold on your thoughts in this alphabet-emblem stiletto from Christian Louboutin. The letters are as obscure as the references you pluck from your vast mental database. Hard to read? Yes both you and the shoe would fit that category—a badge of honor in your book, since novelty ranks high among the erudites you roll with.

Kick It Up NOVEL, CULTURED, INTELLIGENT   **Step It Down** ELITIST, ALOOF

August 29

If there is a method to every display of madness, you will be the one to unearth it. You are a keen analyzer of details—right down to the microscopic level. You dwell in the land of organized chaos, classifying, coding, and creating processes like a cool-headed scientist. Yet no one could accuse you of being formulaic—you're far too inventive for that! Like this Yves St. Laurent wedge, you know that being linear does not have to equate with boring predictability. The rays of gold and silver wind beguilingly into crisscrossed straps. In a spirit similar to your own, they create a uniform language that is at once both orderly and sensuous.

Sign ★ VIRGO

Kick It Up SCIENTIFIC, ORGANIZED, STRATEGIC   *Step It Down* CONTROLLING, COMPULSIVE

August 30

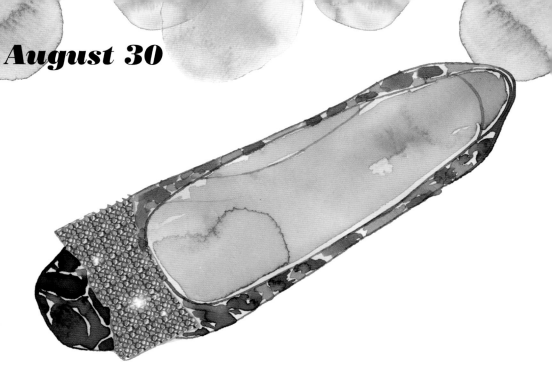

Sensible, steadfast, and systematic, you are the engine that keeps the machine running. With your kittenish charms, you're more prone to purring than to clanking when it comes to getting the job done. This Kate Spade "Noelle" ballet flat says "nice girl" all the way, and you don't mind when people accuse you of being a Goody Two-Shoes. Indeed, it's your sweet feminine wiles that help you expedite your plans and projects—and once you reel 'em in, you keep 'em eating out of the palm of your hand. The faceted jewels of the crystal-encrusted bow wink when lit up, a nod to your secretly sassy nature that only your closest friends will be privy to. Meow!

Kick It Up CHARMING, SWEET, SENSIBLE   ***Step It Down*** RESERVED, CALCULATING

August 31

You are lively, vital, and influential, and the current of life flows through you, pollinating anyone who you come into contact with. You believe in the power of abundance and regeneration—and like this flower- and feather-embellished Valentino sandal, you have the birds and the bees on your side. An irrepressible creatrix, your moods are intoxicating. You can perfume the air with hope when you turn on your cheery optimism. A bit of an attention seeker, you flourish when all eyes are on you.

Sign ★ VIRGO

Kick It Up CREATIVE, OPTIMISTIC, ENTERTAINING   ***Step It Down*** EXAGGERATED, PUSHY

Virgo August 24–September 22

SEP·
TEM·
BER

September 23–October 22 *Libra*

September 1

Like an iron fist in a velvet glove, you use a softer touch while remaining fully in command. Such is the spirit of this chic power loafer by Alexander Wang. The office-appropriate style is all business, while the metallic-pink hue brings a candy-sweet charm. Fittingly, you also have the ability to take fringe ideas and turn them into straightforward concepts, which makes them accessible to the masses without losing their edge.

Sign ★ VIRGO

Kick It Up CONCEPTUAL, ORGANIZED, CHIC ***Step It Down*** STERN, UNYIELDING

September 2

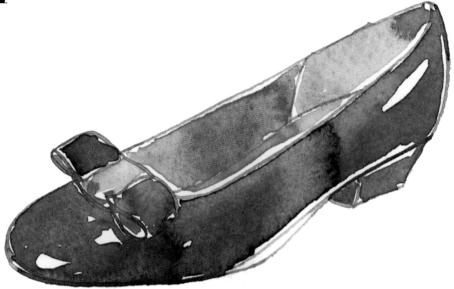

Frills don't bring the thrills in your universe. You prefer the clean, simple elegance of this classic Ferragamo low-heeled pump. Utterly ladylike with the designer's signature bow, there is a sense of propriety and dignity about this shoe. Considering how many pots you like to keep your hands in, it's also appropriately versatile both in heel height and in the classic navy hue. Here's one thing both you and the shoe can clearly demonstrate: stunning simplicity is a beautiful concept . . . and it's harder to pull off than most people realize.

Kick It Up DIGNIFIED, VERSATILE, APPROPRIATE   *Step It Down* STUFFY, RIGHTEOUS

Is beauty only skin deep? Not in the instance of this snakeskin Valentino sandal, nor in the case of you. While you're certainly easy on the eyes, you draw from a deep internal arsenal of powers when people mistakenly assume that you're merely another pretty face. Shock value, in doses, is your secret weapon for getting your way. A bit mysterious, you aren't unbuckled easily. Like the studded accents on this sandal, your exterior can be as tough as it is striking.

Kick It Up STRIKING, NOVEL, STRATEGIC   *Step It Down* ABRASIVE, CLOSED-OFF

September 4

"Architecture is inhabited sculpture," said legendary artist Constantin Brancusi. The same could be said of this Balenciaga sandal. With its mixed material and structured form, it reflects your talent for both art and engineering. You're not satisfied with things that simply look good. You want them well built too! Figuring out how the pieces fit together is one of your obsessions. A structure fanatic, you can spot the weak links in the system and fortify them with your keen problem-solving abilities. You're not afraid to rip something up and start from scratch if it doesn't meet your exacting—yet admirable—standards.

Kick It Up STRUCTURED, SHARP, LOGICAL   *Step It Down* RIGID, PESSIMISTIC

September 5

With the sweet virtue of a blushing bride, you possess an irrefutable sense of romanticism. You'd rather view the world through a gauzy lens than a harsh filter any day. The peach-hued satin of these 1950s Dior wedding slippers requires careful guarding, lest it be sullied with stains. To maintain your dreamy outlook on life, you too prefer to steer clear of harsh elements that disrupt your delicate sensibilities. You're at your finest when weaving projects and plans that are always as intricate, fanciful, and as full of sparkle as the hand beading of these pumps.

Sign ★ VIRGO

Kick It Up IMAGINATIVE, ROMANTIC, PURE   *Step It Down* SHELTERED, UNREALISTIC

September 6

What, exactly, is the definition of *normal?* You might not fly your freak flag high in the sky, but you're hardly predictable. Like these clever oxfords from Osborn Shoes, half of you prefers to slip under the radar, blending in with everyday people. But then a happy interference arrives named Pure Genius. For this portion of your soul, being incognito will never do. Go ahead! Make ripples in the pond like the bright ikat fabric embellishing the heel and toe. It's a fact: unleashing your pent-up notions (and emotions) is the healthiest thing you can do for yourself.

Kick It Up INNOVATIVE, ASTUTE, POISED   *Step It Down* REPRESSED, INCOGNITO

September 7

You belong at the peak of the highest mountains. Sure, the air may be thin and the trek perilous, but you just can't beat the view. Like this fashionable twist on the traditional shearling-lined hiking boot, you were built to go the distance, reaching the apex every time you set a lofty goal. The pronounced wedge reminds fellow climbers that you're ambitious *and* stylish. Just a word to the wise, dear hiker: it can get lonely at the top. Inviting a companion along for the journey might slow your pace, but it will make your accomplishments a thousand times sweeter to celebrate.

Sign ★ VIRGO

Kick It Up AMBITIOUS, FEARLESS, RESILIENT   ***Step It Down*** OBSESSIVE, LONELY

September 8

With its white leather exterior, this Jeffrey Campbell wedge has a light, bright feel. Similarly, you read as a lively and free-spirited optimist who charms with her sunshine-sweet smile. But peel back the layers, and there's a far more abiding quality to be found, much like the sturdy black pump built into this shoe. You're both a party girl and a planner, a creative soul with a can-do spirit. This duality makes you a force to be reckoned with. Not only do you dream up the near impossible, but you actually pull it off . . . with style and integrity to boot.

Sign ★ VIRGO

Kick It Up CREATIVE, STRUCTURED, OPTIMISTIC   ***Step It Down*** OVERCOMMITTED, BURNT OUT

September 9

Challenges? Bring 'em on, sayeth you; or else you'll just seek them out yourself. You love the thrill of mastering a new skill. Usually that means practicing tirelessly until you achieve your daunting goal. Simply walking in these stiltlike crimson platforms—Alexander McQueen's inventive spin on the Mary Jane—might qualify as a trial by fire. They are not for the faint of heart, but they have just the daring lure to draw you in. At times, friends may wonder why you make life so difficult for yourself. The answer is simple: you just hate being bored!

Kick It Up SKILLFUL, DEDICATED, DARING   *Step It Down* SELF-DESTRUCTIVE, COMPLICATED

September 10

This English riding boot might be fine for jumping and posting, but it's also stylishly appropriate for a gentle gait. Grounded, easygoing, and sweet, you prefer the magic of the slower-paced life. Without all that rushing, you actually have time to stop and smell the floribundas, wander through sweetgrasses, and simply connect to your environment. The refined and granular details that might be missed at a faster clip are what you adeptly master—even if that means riding down a long and winding road. When intrigued, you're a dedicated workhorse. For you, the journey is the focus, far more so than the destination.

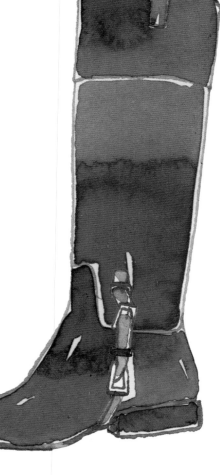

Kick It Up CURIOUS, EASYGOING, DETAIL-ORIENTED **Step It Down** LETHARGIC, MYOPIC

September 11

Is it possible to be both stable and exciting at once? Yes! You are out to prove just that, much like this structured Miu Miu bootie. The silver sparkle says, "Hello, my name is Dynamo," and let's face it . . . you love to wow people upon first encounter, even stirring up some playful controversy with your teasing words. The dynamically arched heel reflects your refusal to fall into the straight-and-narrow camp, and yet it is surprisingly stable. Ankle straps? Perhaps an unnecessary precaution, but you're like that too: for every daring step you take, you always make sure that you and your loved ones are safe and sound.

Kick It Up EXCITING, DYNAMIC, WISE   *Step It Down* OVERLY PRACTICAL, CONTRADICTORY

September 12

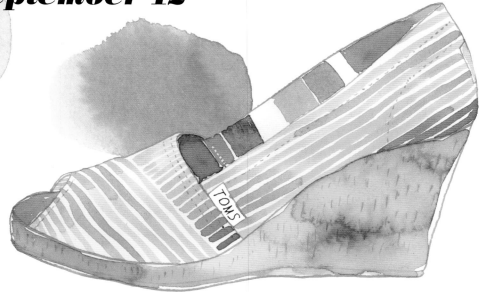

A **woman of conviction,** you float through life with your ethical values intact. This red nautical wedge from TOMS is footwear with a faithful mission. For each pair purchased, the company donates a new pair of shoes to a child in need—perfectly in step with your desire to make the world a better place. A born efficiency expert, you like to create smooth sailing for everyone in your midst. The footprint you'll leave behind will be a long-lasting legacy, as you prefer to teach a girl to fish than bait the hook for her.

Kick It Up PRINCIPLED, CHARITABLE, EFFICIENT   *Step It Down* BOSSY, RIGHTEOUS

"**My Adidas cuts the sand of a foreign land.** With mic in hand, I cold took command." So rhymed rap supergroup Run-DMC about the experience of wearing this classic pair of kicks. Resilient, adventurous, and determined to reach the top, you never have a dull moment in your perpetually active life. Sitting in the stands and watching other people play is so not your thing! Not with all of that wanderlust. You want to be down on the court, fully engaged in the game of life, inevitably getting promoted to captain of the team.

Kick It Up ADVENTUROUS, RESPONSIBLE, ACTIVE   *Step It Down* UNGROUNDED, CUTTHROAT

September 14

These nineteenth-century French evening shoes were a symbol of status during their time. Worn by the well heeled during a time of uprising, they distinguished the wearer from the average citizen. You bear similar markings, thanks to your poise and intuitive understanding of what is appropriate. As such, you regularly find yourself rubbing shoulders with the high-powered types. Although you love your fineries, you realize that all that glitters is not gold. When your efforts to change the system from within don't do the trick, "*Vive la révolution!*" becomes your rallying cry.

Kick It Up POISED, GLAMOROUS, STRATEGIC   *Step It Down* ELITIST, MATERIALISTIC

September 15

You love the finer things in life, especially when they are adorned with sartorial flair. Like this jewel-encrusted Alexander McQueen evening shoe, you have an inimitable sparkle. The imaginative platform clearly announces that Someone Important has stepped into the room. You're less concerned, however, with taking center stage. Your magic lies in boosting other talented souls into the limelight, teaching them to up their standards and to learn to expect the best from themselves—and the world at large.

Sign ★ VIRGO

Kick It Up GLAMOROUS, BENEVOLENT, CHARMED **Step It Down** PERFECTIONISTIC, CODEPENDENT

September 16

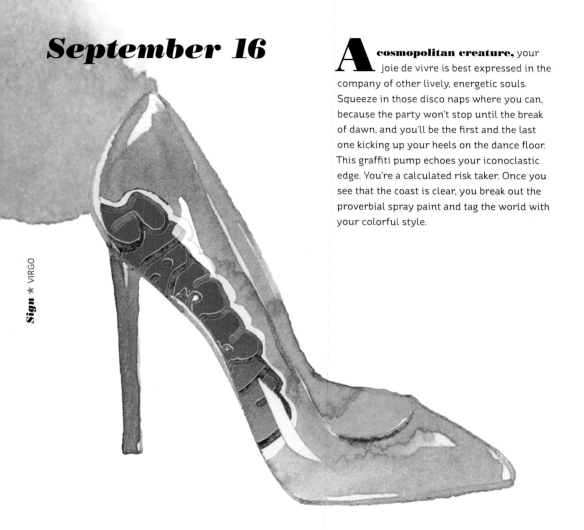

A cosmopolitan creature, your joie de vivre is best expressed in the company of other lively, energetic souls. Squeeze in those disco naps where you can, because the party won't stop until the break of dawn, and you'll be the first and the last one kicking up your heels on the dance floor. This graffiti pump echoes your iconoclastic edge. You're a calculated risk taker. Once you see that the coast is clear, you break out the proverbial spray paint and tag the world with your colorful style.

Kick It Up FREETHINKING, FUN-LOVING, ENERGETIC   *Step It Down* REBELLIOUS, OVER-THE-TOP

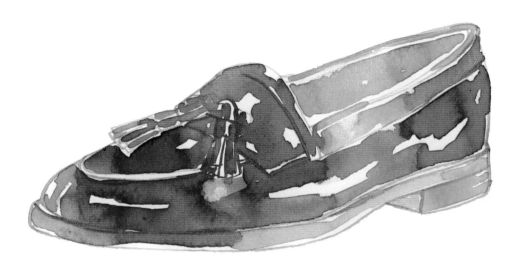

Being understated is highly underrated, as far as you're concerned. This classic tasseled loafer might not scream "attention seeker!" but, hey, fighting for the spotlight is so not your style. You prefer to make your impact from behind the scenes. Self-contained, you do your best work on your own. It's not like you need anyone looking over your shoulder. When you've committed yourself to accomplishing a goal, you work with unflagging dedication toward your ends. Managing the moving parts of a project is just one of your many strengths.

Kick It Up EFFICIENT, ENDURING, EFFECTIVE   *Step It Down* RECLUSIVE, SHY

September 18

A lover of all things beautiful— and a breathtaking creature yourself—you are happiest when dwelling in a world of elegance and luxury. Like the rich dark velvet of this pump, you are layered and a tad mysterious. It's not like you to give away all your secrets. In equal measure, you find yourself both admired and envied for your cool composure. That said, your nature can be as delicate as this shoe's pink satin bow, so you need to steer clear of situations that are overly stressful or intense.

Kick It Up GRACEFUL, INTRIGUING, BEAUTIFUL   **Step It Down** CRYPTIC, ANXIOUS

September 19

"**If only for the sake of elegance,** I try to remain morally pure," quipped French novelist Marcel Proust. This is fitting in your universe, as you are both a stylish sophisticate and a highly principled person. Like this snow-white Valentino chaussure, you keep your life visibly pristine—both on the exterior surface and in the way you conduct your private affairs. But morally chaste you are not: like the festive bow, adorned with gleaming crystals, you're not afraid to add a dash of flash to all that you do.

Sign ★ VIRGO

Kick It Up PRINCIPLED, PURE-HEARTED, DAZZLING   ***Step It Down*** CENSORED, ELITIST

September 20

Luxury and fast-paced living don't always make the happiest of bedfellows. Yet, like these black-and-gold Chanel platform pumps, you merge the two with aplomb. Versatile? That's an understatement. You're a lover and a great organizer of people. Eternally dreaming up projects and plans, you have trouble sitting still for long. Inevitably, your tireless drive kicks in, and you're off to govern another ambitious venture—all while maintaining the utmost in standard and taste.

Kick It Up OPULENT, CAPABLE, DRIVEN   **Step It Down** SCATTERED, EXHAUSTIVE

September 21

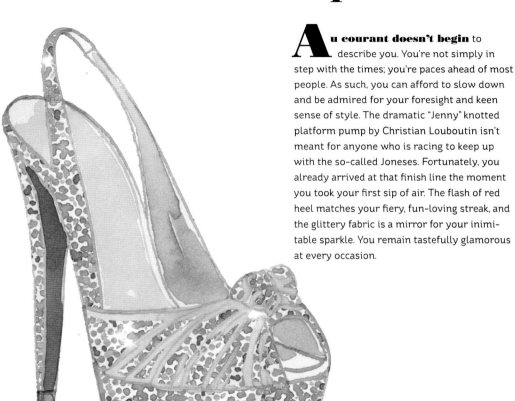

Au courant doesn't begin to describe you. You're not simply in step with the times; you're paces ahead of most people. As such, you can afford to slow down and be admired for your foresight and keen sense of style. The dramatic "Jenny" knotted platform pump by Christian Louboutin isn't meant for anyone who is racing to keep up with the so-called Joneses. Fortunately, you already arrived at that finish line the moment you took your first sip of air. The flash of red heel matches your fiery, fun-loving streak, and the glittery fabric is a mirror for your inimitable sparkle. You remain tastefully glamorous at every occasion.

Sign ★ VIRGO

Kick It Up TRENDSETTING, GLAMOROUS, PERCEPTIVE　***Step It Down*** GLIB, JUDGMENTAL

September 22

Your untamed heart will not be corralled. Nope, you have far too much joie de vivre to let anyone fence you in. Surely, if you were to name a power animal, the wild stallion would be your totem. This Alexander Wang boot radiates that very spirit. With its horsehair adornment, each step you take is akin to whipping your mane in the wind. People don't always know what to make of you at first glance—at times, you may seem downright intimidating. Once you deem people trustworthy enough to join your herd, however, you'll lead the charge to adventure and remain a true companion for life.

Kick It Up EXCITING, LOYAL, FIERCE   *Step It Down* STORMY, DESTRUCTIVE

September 23

Like these punched-leather ballet flats, you're a total breakout star. People are often surprised by your swift and sudden actions, which generally delight and entertain. For you, actions speak louder than words. You're not one to sit around and complain about the barriers that are holding you back. No, you'd rather figure out a way to get around them or fell them with the sheer might of your persistence. A true dynamo, your creativity and wild instincts will attract many fascinating people into your universe.

Sign ★ LIBRA

Kick It Up DYNAMIC, ACTION-ORIENTED, ENTERTAINING ***Step It Down*** RASH, CARELESS

September 24

Sign ★ LIBRA

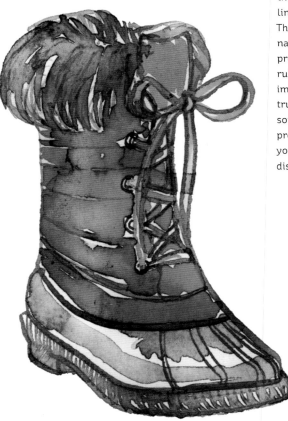

By land or by sea, you're willing to trek the distance to explore the whims of your rich imagination. This lined boot has "pioneer" written all over it. The sturdy leather matches your resilient nature, while the thick wool lining keeps you protected from the elements. And like the rubber sole, you are known to have a bit of an impenetrable shell at times. This is especially true when you've made up your mind to do something daring. You know your ideas will probably freak most people out, but when your compass is pointing north, you can't be dissuaded from your divinely guided mission.

Kick It Up PIONEERING, STRONG, DARING   *Step It Down* HOTHEADED, STUBBORN

September 25

They say that the best-laid schemes of mice and men often go awry. Well, that's a chance you're willing to take. An imaginative and exacting strategist, there's a bit of a mad genius living inside of you. Going against the grain happens to be your field of specialty; and like these Marc Jacobs mouse flats, you do so with a twist of tongue-in-cheek humor. Like the punk-inspired studs dotting the surface of the leather, you can be prickly when people question your methods. Rules, as far as you're concerned, were meant to be mastered—so that they can be broken more effectively, of course.

Sign ★ LIBRA

Kick It Up PRECISE, VISIONARY, MASTERFUL   ***Step It Down*** RADICAL, CYNICAL

September 26

Sign ★ LIBRA

Like the stacked heel and structured straps on this architectural sandal, you like it best when things take a clear and defined shape. The elemental hues of black and cream speak to your love of stark and elegant simplicity. And like the intricacy and individuality of its form, you are self-assured enough to make a bold public statement when it's time to express yourself. Technically oriented, you are a realist at heart, but that doesn't mean you aren't creative. Facts are the building blocks of your success. Art is the signature flourish that you bring to all that you do.

Kick It Up STRUCTURED, CONFIDENT, BRIGHT **Step It Down** AGGRESSIVE, UPTIGHT

September 27

Cool and composed, you are a true classic, perfectly pooled with this "Something Blue" pump from Manolo Blahnik. Like the sensual curve of the heel, you arch elegantly to new heights. The crystal buckle mirrors your love of luxury, and the rich blue tone and form of the shoe are both allusions to romantic nuptials. You're not afraid to make a wholehearted commitment, although you need time to deliberate before you can truly be wedded to any person, place, or idea. While you'll never let the world see you struggle, beneath your Jackie-O smile beats the heart of a perfectionist. Learn to be gentler with yourself so your mood doesn't wind up matching the hue of this shoe.

Sign ★ LIBRA

Kick It Up SENSUAL, HIGH-MINDED, LUXURIOUS *Step It Down* PEDANTIC, MOODY

September 28

Like this Betsey Johnson peep-toe, your feline magnetism is your greatest charm. A minx to the core, you definitely know how to work your allure to your advantage. People are generally so dazzled by your presence that the thought of saying no to you simply never crosses their minds. Your passion for life burns as brightly as the signature hot-pink hue splashed on the underside of the shoe. You let it peek out regularly, stirring up excitement with every step you take. Valentines? Admirers? You'll have many in this lifetime, perhaps too many to count.

Sign ★ LIBRA

Kick It Up CHARISMATIC, PASSIONATE, DAZZLING   ***Step It Down*** CUNNING, OPPORTUNISTIC

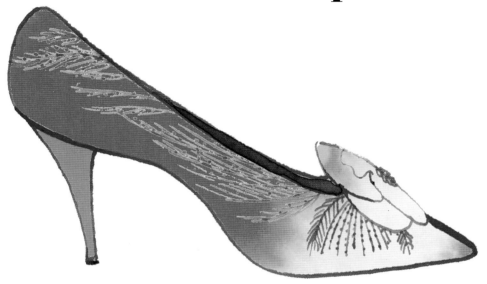

Nothing says **"goddess"** like a pair of vintage Dior heels, and that you truly are. Femininity becomes you—and rumor has it your blood runs pink. A delicate silk flower, intricate beading, adorning feathers: you are all about the details, the more gorgeous the better. The arts appeal to you, and you're as much an appreciator and advocate as you are a creatrix. You understand that beauty can create a powerful charge, one that moves people on a deeply subconscious level. It is your answer to world peace and the weapon you use to disarm your opponents.

Kick It Up ARTSY, DYNAMIC, DETAIL-ORIENTED   *Step It Down* IMAGE-CONSCIOUS, SLY

September 30

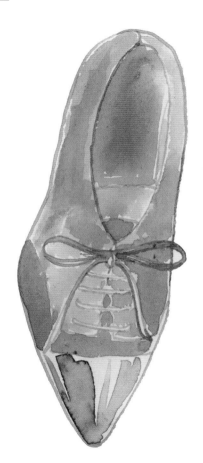

Michael Kors designed this "Truman Capote" oxford as an homage to the man who shares your birthday. Like the brilliantly eccentric author, you are solidly opinionated and not afraid to speak your truths. Your views can be as pointed as the steely toe of this shoe, but somehow you manage to express them without losing friends. That's because, like the mirrored surface, you are generally reflecting the unavoidable truth right back to them. Your wit and candor are matched by your perennial style, making you a shoe-in for the jet set. Raise the red velvet ropes. Why yes, you *are* on the list.

Kick It Up INGENIOUS, AUTHENTIC, WISE   ***Step It Down*** TACTLESS, ARGUMENTATIVE

September 23–October 22 *Libra*

OCTO·
BER

October 23–November 21 *Scorpio*

October 1

Where's the soiree ce soir? You're a social butterfly who comes to life in the company of refined and elegant intellectuals. Like this 1914 French evening shoe, you are at your finest after sunset, when the glow of ambient lighting casts life in a romantic hue. The shoe's basic black undercarriage is simple and sturdy, just as you are by nature a reliable soul. With its gorgeous brocade of lace, however, this shoe is anything but ordinary. A sensualist and artiste, you are captivated by the beauty of life's finer things and will appreciate them greatly throughout your lifetime.

Kick It Up OUTGOING, SENSUAL, INTELLECTUAL   *Step It Down* HIGHBROW, GLIB

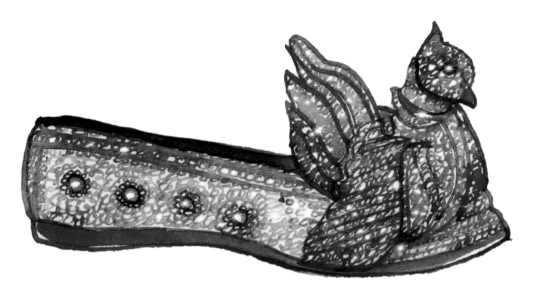

The royal hintha bird adorning this late-nineteenth-century Burmese coronation shoe symbolizes loyalty, a respect for traditional values, stability, and prosperity. You are a similar icon for those who adore you. You're the wise oracle they turn to for guidance, the rock that they lean on. The bird's penetrating gaze stares right into the soul, just as you use your eyes to form a deep and knowing connection. Like ceremonial garb, this elaborate slipper is embroidered with metallic thread and adorned with sequins, beads, and cut glass. Special occasions are your specialty, particularly when you can connect them to a sacred and meaningful purpose.

Kick It Up WISE, SOULFUL, INTIMATE   *Step It Down* SOLEMN, HEAVY

October 3

What appears simple at first glance is often a complex blend of elements that are woven together seamlessly. That's you in a nutshell. Like this navy, white, and tan pump, you are an apothecary of style, and your signature brew is tasteful, traditional, and chic. As such, you remain in step with au courant trends while simultaneously emanating timeless grace. In short, you are pure paradox; a thoroughly modern old soul. Creating beauty in the world is one of your unique gifts, and you are quite the discerning collector of *objets*. You're willing to sacrifice comfort for style, if it means creating a striking and inspiring visual for others to behold.

Kick It Up GRACE, LEADERSHIP, BROAD-MINDEDNESS   **Step It Down** OVERCOMMITTING, MATERIALISTIC

You might use a soft touch, but you have a firm grasp on exactly what you want from life. The petal-pink blush of this leather Dior sandal is disarmingly sweet. Similarly, you know how to pour on the sugar, charming your unsuspecting targets into happily doing your bidding. With its delicate gold studs, the bondage-inspired tassel is a small giveaway to your undercover bossy streak. Thankfully, you're a gracious leader who keeps everyone's best interests at heart.

Sign ★ LIBRA

Kick It Up CHARMING, PURPOSEFUL, DIPLOMATIC   *Step It Down* MANIPULATIVE, DOMINATING

October 5

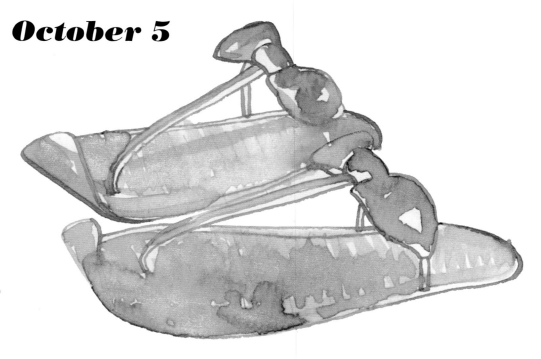

Regal, authoritative, and just, leadership comes naturally to you. Your coolheaded wisdom is your guiding force. On principle, you strive to understand both sides of an argument before passing judgment. These pharaoh's sandals are artifacts of ancient Egypt and were worn by King Tut himself. They are modest in design, just as you prefer to keep a somewhat low profile. Still, luxury always makes its way to your door. Tutankhamen's sandals are made of pure gold—which is also a reflection of your compassionate, loving heart.

Kick It Up FAIR-MINDED, REGAL, COMPASSIONATE   *Step It Down* DETACHED, SEVERE

October 6

Active, curious, and on the move, you're a hard one to pin down. This quirky platform sneaker from Jeffrey Campbell has your fun-loving spring in its step. A lover of music and the arts, you are happiest when surrounded by beauty. The pursuit of pleasure is of the highest order to you. You want to enjoy every last drop of goodness that life has to offer and to share the love with your ever-widening circle of friends. You have a technical side as well. Like the heel's stacked, symmetrical layers, you're able to distill situations to their black-and-white essence, which makes you an excellent problem solver and judge.

Kick It Up FUN, DECADENT, TECHNICAL   *Step It Down* FLIGHTY, OVERINDULGENT

October 7

Like the orange-and-turquoise ridges adorning these cowboy ankle boots, your life is a series of peaks and valleys. A seeker, philosopher queen, and rebel rolled into one, your Libran scales have been known to swing between extremes. Taking chances is what makes you feel alive, especially when your quest is connected to a humanitarian mission. The body of this shoe is both rugged and sleek, just as you manage to be resilient without losing your stylish cool. A keen and insightful judge, you don't mince words when it comes to giving your viewpoint. You follow your truth over what is considered popular opinion, a rebel at heart.

Kick It Up PHILOSOPHICAL, ATTENTIVE, SHARP   **Step It Down** SCATHING, UNSTABLE

Whoever said **"Don't sweat the small stuff"** was definitely not talking to you! You're obsessed with the details and will work tirelessly to gain a masterful hold over something that most people might consider inconsequential. Your finished product is sure to impress: pure genius! Like the intricate beading on this vintage 1960s Dior pump, the finer points are your specialty. You're both an artist and an engineer, a wonderful combination indeed. The pump's body style is simple and well structured, an echo of your commitment to quality and functionality. The glamorous jewels reveal your love of beauty and your undeniably romantic nature. No wonder your dance card is always full.

Kick It Up HARDWORKING, TALENTED, ROMANTIC   **Step It Down** NITPICKY, FANATICAL

October 9

Sign ★ LIBRA

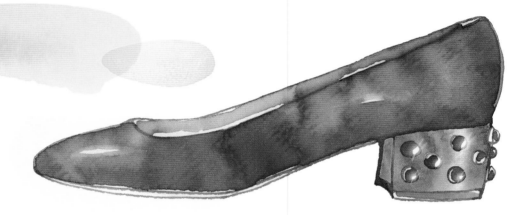

It don't mean a thing if it ain't got that swing, at least as far as you're concerned. The coral Pelosi satin of this Stella McCartney pump is fearlessly vivacious and undeniably fun. It takes a big personality to pull these off, and you've got that. The jeweled heel catches and refracts the light, just as you sparkle when you step into a room. You captivate with your conversations and seduce with your sense of humor. While you don't mind taking center stage, you're no spotlight stealer. You love to share the glory with a partner and are happiest when paired up as half of a dynamic duo.

Kick It Up CAPTIVATING, BRIGHT, GENEROUS   *Step It Down* OSTENTATIOUS, BRASH

October 10

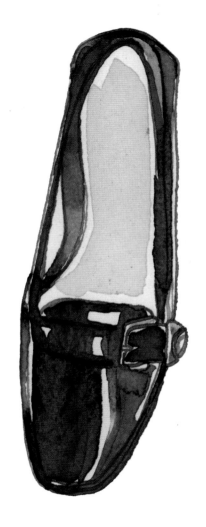

Practical luxury is the name of the game for you. Never wasteful and always tasteful, you know how to make a strong yet simple statement. Like you, this understated Prada driver shoe is the picture of classic cool. Quality is key, and you invest time and money only on things of lasting value. With its menswear-inspired design, it borrows from the boys without apology. Woe betide the person who says women can't do this or that! You'll make it your mission to prove him wrong, and you're likely to one-up him in the process. Who, you, competitive? Well, maybe just a little.

Sign ★ LIBRA

Kick It Up TASTEFUL, COMPETENT, JUST   *Step It Down* CUTTHROAT, RESTRAINED

October 11

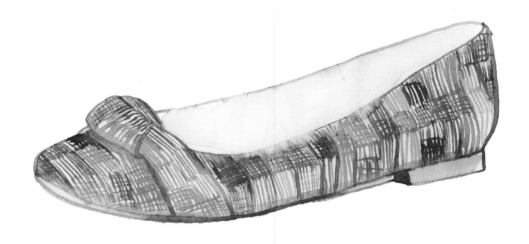

Like the multicolored squares on this Stuart Weitzman "Puffystuff" flat, you are here to experience the full spectrum of life's offerings. Why settle on one flavor when you can enjoy the rainbow? While making firm decisions can be challenging for you, variety is absolutely the spice of your life. With its ruched back, this shoe was designed for comfort, a preferred quality for someone with your easygoing nature and delicate sensibilities. Debris and disharmony can upset your internal balance, and you may shy away from conflict. An optimist, you'd rather approach life in the spirit of birthday mate Eleanor Roosevelt, who said, "It is better to light a candle than to curse the darkness."

Kick It Up CURIOUS, HARMONIOUS, OPTIMISTIC   *Step It Down* INDECISIVE, INSULATED

October 12

The **"Lady Victoria" bootie** from Poetic Licence sends a naughty, tongue-in-cheek wink to an era when modesty and propriety ruled. You're a bawdy lass yourself, a master of the artful tease. You know how to reveal and conceal in just the right measure, which drives your fans wild with desire. In Victorian days, the ankle was considered a seductive body part, and this midcalf boot provides the "appropriate" coverage. Yet the colorful blossoms on the shoe's carpet-style fabric belie decorum. Are you a proper lady or a bona fide wild child? Depends on the day. One thing's for sure: your autobiography is certain to be scintillating!

Sign ★ LIBRA

Kick It Up PLAYFUL, TANTALIZING, IRRESISTIBLE   ***Step It Down*** CONFUSING, DISINGENUOUS

October 13

Structure meets sensuality in this Christian Louboutin loafer pump. That's a hard bridge to gap, but one that's not unfamiliar to you. You are certainly business-like at the heart of it all, and you don't mind formalities one bit. Nevertheless, you always bring a seductive flair to the meeting, as the bright-blue fabric and signature red heel represent. Like the shoe's dramatic platform, you set a high bar for yourself and must be careful not to create impossible standards. Allow yourself to enjoy more luxury too. With its gold-edged throat, this pump manages to be glamorous without ostentation, a line you can walk with aplomb.

Kick It Up PROFESSIONAL, COMPETENT, SENSUAL   **Step It Down** PERFECTIONISTIC, RIGID

October 14

Like this printed camel hair loafer, you are the picture of understated cool. Just a dash of flash is all you need to make a statement. You prefer to work behind the scenes, as you are sensitive to the judgments and critiques of others. Away from the spotlight's glare, you create your works of genius, giving each detail the utmost care and forethought. The repeating diamond shapes decorating this shoe are symmetrical and rhythmic in nature, echoing your Libran desire for order and balance. An avid observer of life, you thrive while traveling, embracing new cultural standards with the same ease it takes to slip into this comfortable loafer.

Kick It Up COOL, CAPABLE, OBSERVANT   *Step It Down* SECRETIVE, STANDOFFISH

October 15

Poetic, romantic, and artistic, you're here to soak up the good life with every fiber of your being. This vintage flapper shoe is a relic of the Roaring Twenties, a time where culture flourished, jazz music blossomed, and women rebelled against restrictive social standards. A delightful rebel, you're never shy about speaking your mind. Like the gold-and-black rays of these shoes, you have an electric dynamism about you, and your effusive personality could fill any room. This shoe's sinuous "Louis heel" was a symbol of upper-class status in its day. With your refined tastes, it's only natural for you to travel in elegant circles, rubbing shoulders with society's elite.

Kick It Up JOYFUL, EFFUSIVE, REFINED   **Step It Down** EXTRAVAGANT, ELITIST

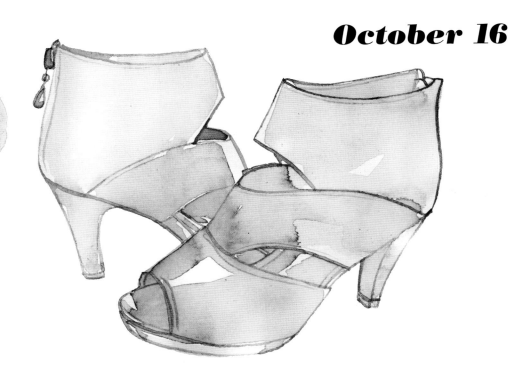

Like these chic Coach sandals, you are a woman of impeccable tastes. You're not only an arbiter of style but also a stellar sounding board for anyone looking for a fair, well-considered opinion. Gracious and diplomatic, you know how to assert yourself while still remaining as delicate as the seashell-pink tone of these shoes. Because of your ability to see both sides of a matter, you are sometimes a contradiction unto yourself. The enclosed leather panels and revealing cutaways play to this paradox, mirroring your own duality. Your good sense always prevails, helping you strike a fair and judicious balance in any situation.

Kick It Up STYLISH, WISE, JUDICIOUS   *Step It Down* RESTRAINED, FUSSY

October 17

"**I did not have everything from life.** I've had too much!" gushed silver screen starlet Rita Hayworth, who shares your birthday. You're a no-limits lady yourself, eager and willing to enjoy all of life's luscious offerings. Stuart Weitzman's forties-era "Retro Rose" T-strap is a nod to your abundant—and sometimes hedonistic—approach to life. Valued at $1 million, this shoe's ornamental flower is encrusted with over eighteen hundred Kwiat diamonds and weighs in at around one hundred carats. You're quite the jewel yourself: glamorous, glittering with dramatic flair, and so much fun to be around. It's no wonder that luxury, and the people who enjoy it, inevitably find their way to your door.

Kick It Up LUXURIOUS, ABUNDANT, OPEN-MINDED   **Step It Down** HEDONISTIC, MATERIALISTIC

October 18

Twirl on, sister! Like the majorettes who march in these boots, you love having multiple "batons" in the air. A true Renaissance woman, you have far too many interests to focus on just one. Although you've been known to exhaust yourself with your passions, your unflagging optimism shores you up time and again. You have stellar stage presence too, and you know how to keep the crowds pumped. A natural leader, you dance in the wind like the boot's tassels, fun and free spirited to the core.

Sign ★ LIBRA

Kick It Up MULTIFACETED, PASSIONATE, OPTIMISTIC   *Step It Down* OVERCOMMITTED, BURNT OUT

October 19

Like this black babydoll peep-toe pump from the late 1930s, you've got class and sass in equal measure. A sprinkling of studs lights up the basic black fabric. Similarly, you're a master of surprises. You enjoy it when people underestimate you, which can happen when you fly under the radar for too long. Like a peacock fanning his feathers, the colorful scalloping around the toe reveals the truth: when you're ready to strut your stuff, you're anything but ordinary. You can outshine the competition with a simple splash of your colorful personality— that is, should you be charmed enough to reveal your wild side.

Kick It Up SURPRISING, ELEGANT, SASSY   *Step It Down* DEFIANT, MISLEADING

October 20

A born trendsetter, you couldn't care less about keeping up with the Joneses. In fact, the Joneses are trying to keep up with you. This stunning pink Yves St. Laurent heel makes a fearless style statement. Bright and poppy, this shoe draws stares—just as you do with your colorful ideas and avant-garde expression. While your imagination soars to distant galaxies, you manage to keep one perfectly centered foot in the material plane. The mirrored gold plate reflects your love of luxury, while the classic loafer cut is a nod to your respect for tradition. Yours is a balance that few can strike, which is why you are often imitated but never duplicated.

Kick It Up CUTTING EDGE, FASHIONABLE, ORIGINAL   *Step It Down* COMPETITIVE, SHALLOW

October 21

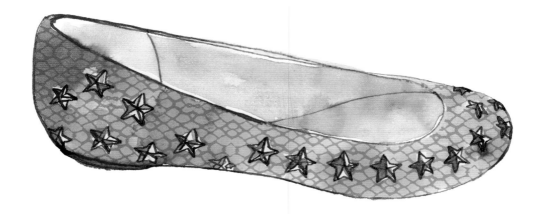

Enchanting and magnetic, you cast a spell on all who come in contact with you. People learn to expect the unexpected from you, mesmerized by your moves. The snake-embossed leather of this Jimmy Choo "Western Star" studded ballet flat is a nod to your ability to shed your skin and regenerate, season after season, year after year. Like the silver stud embellishments, you're a star in your own right. Highly entertaining, you put on a great show. That's because you're willing to share the full range of your expression with the world—from the highs to the lows, and everything in between.

Kick It Up MESMERIZING, ADAPTIVE, ENTERTAINING **Step It Down** ILLUSORY, DRAMATIC

Sensual and captivating, this vintage Dolce and Gabbana evening shoe simmers with your seductive allure. "Your words are my food, your breath my wine. You are everything to me," said legendary actress Sarah Bernhardt, born today. You're a hopeless romantic, caught up in the rapture of love. You happily sashay through the courtship dance with your many fascinating suitors. Like this shoe's gemstone embellishment, you enjoy life's finer things, especially when they come gift wrapped. Your caring heart also sparkles like a jewel. "Life begets life. Energy begets energy. It is by spending oneself that one becomes rich," said Bernhardt. As a woman who gives her all, you'd simply have to agree.

Sign ★ LIBRA

Kick It Up SEDUCTIVE, ROMANTIC, COMPASSIONATE   ***Step It Down*** LOVESICK, SPOILED

October 23

Fasten your seat belt; it's going to be a thrilling ride. With layers of buckles, this quirky Jeffrey Campbell bootie keeps you safely strapped in. Good thing, since your adventure-seeking nature often leads you into daredevil terrain. You believe in living life on the edge; there's nothing halfway about you. Your passion—and sometimes your temper—burns as brightly as the shoe's crimson hue. Sexy, feisty, and even a little bit bossy, you see yourself as above it all, rising up like the thick and defiant platform heel. If it's not a challenge, it's just a waste of your time.

Kick It Up ADVENTUROUS, BRIGHT, FEISTY   *Step It Down* BRASH, RECKLESS

Life without dramatic arcs and flourishes is simply too boring for you to consider. With its sinuous form and layered, fanlike throat, this 1930s Steven Arpad pump is reminiscent of a dragon. Supernatural symbols, dragons are masters of transformation, just like you. You're capable of slipping in and out of many roles, a versatile creature indeed. Like the metallic pattern on this pump, you are a lover of details. You'll work tirelessly to master your craft so that your capabilities become a match for your impressive outer image.

October 24

Sign ★ SCORPIO

Kick It Up THEATRICAL, VERSATILE, MASTERFUL   *Step It Down* HAUGHTY, SUPERFICIAL

October 25

The Cubist art movement—pioneered by your birthday mate Pablo Picasso—attempted to capture energy visually. Similarly, you view life from unusual angles, picking up on hidden clues and motions. With a block heel that extends behind the body of the shoe, this Jeffrey Campbell "Security" bootie visually expresses the moment between each step. Those tiny transitional beats are missed by most—but not you. You are fascinated by fluctuations and love to help walk people through their personal evolutions. Said Picasso, "Everything you can imagine is real." That includes balancing on this seemingly precarious shoe, but with your strategic mind, you have a gift for finding stability where most people stumble.

Kick It Up SENSITIVE, INTUITIVE, BALANCED   *Step It Down* OVERINVOLVED, SUSPICIOUS

Calm, cool, and crisp, you are all business, comfortable with the idea of large numbers of people depending upon you. Like these muted metallic ballet flats, you shine without being ostentatious. The gold-and-bronze fibers of this shoe are woven together in neat succession, mirroring your talent for organizing the threads of a project into a tight, cohesive unit. While you don't mind a decorative flourish such as the ribbon detail on the shoe's toe, you prefer to keep your feet planted in the practical zone. You're alluring without trying, and there's something undeniably seductive about your take-charge ways.

Kick It Up CAPABLE, ORGANIZED, ALLURING   ***Step It Down*** DEMANDING, ICY

October 27

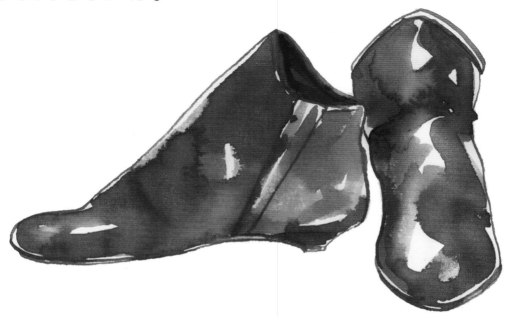

Dynamic, bright, and impulsive, these adorable red pixie boots were made for your feet. Like a winged and magical fairy, you're a bit of a mischief maker, waking people up from their slumbering ennui with your provocative style. You're as kittenish as the kitten heel when your playful side takes the helm. Relics of the 1980s—an era of vivid and voracious self-expression—this boot is a nod to your envelope-pushing style. You can always be counted on to bring a "New Wave" of ideas and energy to any given situation. If you stir the pot in the process, that's all the better.

Kick It Up MAGICAL, PROVOCATIVE, INVENTIVE **Step It Down** RABBLE-ROUSING, TEMPERAMENTAL

October 28

Precise and intricate, the flame stitch embroidery of this 1750s latchet shoe required a level of mastery to create. With your devotion to the details, you're no stranger to this realm. You have impeccable tastes and exacting standards, but you don't demand anything that you're not willing to give in return. You're willing to work humbly alongside the experts to hone your expertise. The shoe's gold silk heel was highly unusual for its time, a nod to your love of the rare and obscure. The shoe's curved "Louis heel" was reserved for the upper class in its day, and with your talent for attracting money, those very echelons are calling your name.

Kick It Up IMPECCABLE, HARDWORKING, PROSPEROUS *Step It Down* PICKY, RUTHLESS

October 29

Like the stark-white leather of this vintage 1980s bootie, there's nothing you love more than a clean canvas to create upon. Where others see emptiness, you see pure possibility. You're a master of making something from nothing, leaving people spellbound in the process. The flame-shaped pieces fanning the throat of this shoe are as white-hot as your creativity. Your ideas may be ahead of their time, but if you stand on your convictions, they ultimately catch on like wildfire. Like the silver studs bedazzling the shoe, you charm with a simple zing of bling, endearing people with your playful sparkle.

Kick It Up IMAGINATIVE, EDGY, DAZZLING   *Step It Down* FUSSY, MANIPULATIVE

Law and order does not a boring universe make. You understand the purpose of structures, systems, and rules, especially when they foster greater productivity. This military-inspired kitten heel is at once commanding and sexy, perfect for a powerful woman like yourself. Unfurl the maps and hoist the sails. Like explorer Christopher Columbus, born today, you'll happily lead the expedition into new terrain. Even if you veer off course, your wise devotion inspires loyalty in your troops. The metal embellishments of this shoe alludes to the decorating of a general's uniform. In this lifetime, you're bound to be honored for your unflagging service to the ones you love.

Kick It Up POWERFUL, DEVOTED, WISE **Step It Down** IMPERIOUS, MILITANT

October 31

This 1960s Beat poet flat was the attire of a cultural movement, an era of nonconformity and spontaneous creativity. Never one to paint by numbers, you're a true original. Like the colorblocked fabric of this flat, your life is a fascinating patchwork of experiences, culled through the direction of your own curious nature.

Naturally inquisitive, you're drawn to exploring the mysteries that hide in life's shadows. Counterculture and indie movements appeal to your sensibilities, but you must be careful not to let your explorations take you too far down the rabbit hole. Keep a foot in both worlds, and you'll never get tripped up.

Kick It Up EXPERIMENTAL, INDEPENDENT, CURIOUS   **Step It Down** LOST, RECKLESS

October 23 – November 21 *Scorpio*

NO·VEM·BER

November 22 – December 21 *Sagittarius*

November 1

You're no stranger to dancing with danger. Like this pitch-black Yves St. Laurent "Opyum" pump, you are fascinated by the dark and mysterious side of life. A thrillseeker with Bond girl appeal, your fearless quests lead you into all kinds of fascinating adventures. Along with its seductive charm, the chain detail gives this pump an air of authority. You're quite the same way yourself: it's clear that you are the boss of your operations, and few would dare dispute you on that. Nevertheless you are more intoxicating than intimidating. Few can resist the spell you cast, so use your powers for good!

Kick It Up ALLURING, AUTHORITATIVE, COURAGEOUS   **Step It Down** DESTRUCTIVE, DOMINATING

November 2

Like this gorgeous peacock pump from the 1950s, you are glamorous and showy without being over the top. You fan your feathers selectively, always knowing the right time to reveal your magic. Like the peacock, your true colors are definitely of the iridescent variety: they change according to the light. That's not because you're deceptive, but rather because you are too richly versatile to be captured in a single hue. As this elegantly ladylike shoe suggests, you are adept in social situations. With your keen understanding of the human experience, you can transform yourself to be what is needed in any given moment.

Kick It Up GLAMOROUS, MULTIFACETED, ADAPTIVE   *Step It Down* PERPLEXING, WITHHOLDING

November 3

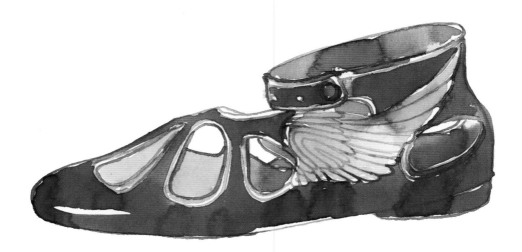

This English swimming shoe emerged in the 1920s, when women were first breaking into the world of competitive sports. An unstoppable warrior queen, you're here to shatter any glass ceilings placed over your head. The trompe l'oeil wings painted on this shoe are a nod to your ability to soar above limitations. Its crimson hue is bright and fierce, just like your unstoppable drive. It's your mission to show the world what you—and all women—are capable of. You thrill at the opportunity to be a contender, and like iconic Vogue editor Anna Wintour, born today, your keen sensibilities can influence the masses.

Kick It Up GROUNDBREAKING, UNSTOPPABLE, ICONIC   *Step It Down* ICY, AGGRESSIVE

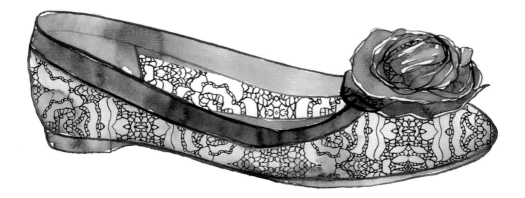

The symbol of sophisticated seduction, a layer of black lace shrouds the precious nude body of this Valentino ballet flat. Similarly, you are prone to concealing your own delicate nature. You would love to bare your soul more often, but alas, the world is not always a gentle enough place for someone as sensitive as you are. Being vulnerable is both your greatest desire and your deepest fear. Like this ballet flat, you sheath yourself in an enigmatic outer layer as a means of self-protection. That untouchable allure only adds to your appeal. You are richly creative and deeply connected to your work. Like the blossom adorning the toe, you enjoy planting seeds and watching them grow.

Kick It Up SEDUCTIVE, COMPASSIONATE, CREATIVE   *Step It Down* SCARED, SUSPICIOUS

November 5

Can one be understated and alluring at the same time? Indeed! And you and this Yves St. Laurent gray suede platform boot are out to prove it. With a nod to the Victorian era, it teases and tantalizes with its enticing modesty. You know how to drop a subtle hint that winds up having the force of an atom bomb. People can't help but be affected by your subliminal cues and behind-the-scenes direction, even if they are unaware of where it came from. The boot's streamlined curves and six-inch heel lend a dash of sex appeal. You always bring a pinch of spice to your recipe for success.

Kick It Up ENTICING, MODEST, SPICY   ***Step It Down*** TEASING, GUARDED

November 6

With its metallic sheen and festive flounce of ribbons, this flirty Kate Spade "Scenic" sandal is ready to fete the evening in celebratory style. You're an irrepressible party girl yourself, a night owl who owns whatever scene you step onto. Jewel-toned straps the color of sapphires echo your love of life's finer things. Being surrounded by art and objects of beauty lifts your spirits, and you may have a talent for creating gorgeous visuals and music yourself. People's spirits lift when you turn on your captivating charisma. You just know how to make people feel good about themselves: a true and powerful gift indeed.

Kick It Up FESTIVE, SCENE-STEALING, UPLIFTING   *Step It Down* DISINGENUOUS, UNGROUNDED

November 7

The swirling paisley pattern on this late-nineteenth-century English tapestry boot has its own complex rhyme and reason. With your scientific mind and detective's curiosity, you are fascinated by life's intricacies. Figuring out how the threads weave together is one of your specialties, and few can match your single-focused determination. Like this Victorian-era boot, you can be rather buttoned-up. Scientist Marie Curie, who was born today, said, "Be less curious about people and more curious about ideas." In spite of your somewhat flamboyant appearance, you are at heart an introvert. True friends know they must earn your trust, but once they do, they are forever part of your delightful inner circle.

Sign ★ SCORPIO

Kick It Up SCIENTIFIC, CLEVER, LUXE   **Step It Down** CLOSED, DISTRUSTFUL

November 8

This python wedge boot from Jimmy Choo shares your hypnotically sexy appeal. It wraps itself beguilingly around the ankle and calf, just as you become closely entwined with the ones you love. You can be a woman of extremes. When it's time to change, you're not afraid to shed your skin and start over. With its distinct markings, this boot is one of a kind, and being an original is important to you. While you don't need to be the flashiest person in the crowd, you like to leave a lingering impression.

Sign ★ SCORPIO

Kick It Up HYPNOTIZING, INTIMATE, BRAVE **Step It Down** IRRATIONAL, VENOMOUS

November 9

The zigzag layers of this Christian Louboutin "Ziggy" bootie follows a trajectory similar to that of your life. In true Scorpio fashion, you embrace the highs and the lows—the more dramatic, the better. Living on the edge is your preference. You want to feel the pounding of your heart, the pulsing of your blood. Glittery hot-pink, purple, silver, and blue patches sparkle with your magical appeal. You've been known to chase after shiny things, following the lure of fantasy rather than giving over to reality. With these sky-high heels, you don't mind keeping your head in the clouds. The view is much more interesting up there, as far as you're concerned.

Kick It Up EXCITING, COLORFUL, DREAMY   *Step It Down* UNREALISTIC, VOLATILE

This pump is a relic of 1938, the year of a major economic crash. Since money was scant, people had to stretch their imaginations and create innovative solutions for everyday needs. With your resourceful brand of genius, you know how to turn the blasé into the brilliant. The austere brown-and-white body of this shoe does not tell its entire story. Resting upon a gold-dipped heel, it bursts into a garden of blossoms at the toe. You're well aware that appearances can be deceiving. Not one to give up without a thorough investigation, you'll mine for the gem in any situation, dreaming up awe-inspiring alternatives that defy probability.

Sign ★ SCORPIO

Kick It Up INGENIOUS, RESOURCEFUL, AWE-INSPIRING   *Step It Down* FRUGAL, OBSESSIVE

November 11

"You can do anything, but lay off of my blue suede shoes," crooned Elvis Presley of his iconic kicks. Call it a warning—or perhaps a threat—but through these shoes, the King sent out a metaphoric message that he was not to be messed with. Nor are you. Fierce, yet feminine, you are an amazing ally and a formidable opponent. You'll fight to the end to protect the ones you love. Loyalty reigns supreme in your universe. With your sterling integrity and unwavering dedication, you are indeed a "true blue" soul whom people trust unflinchingly.

Kick It Up LOYAL, PROTECTIVE, TRUSTWORTHY   **Step It Down** COMBATIVE, CLIQUISH

November 12

"**I am always busy,** which is perhaps the chief reason why I am always well," quipped women's rights activist Elizabeth Cady Stanton, who shares your birthday. Like you, she was a fearless fighter who never backed down from her beliefs. With its feline stripes and red-slashed heel, Christian Louboutin's "Bicho" stiletto is a nod to your jungle cat fierceness. Always on the move, you have the spirit of a prowling tigress. Your opponents had best watch their backs! Strategic, intelligent, and ahead of the curve, you can hold your prey captive without lifting a finger. Channel that power toward a good cause, and you might just start a revolution of your own.

Sign ★ SCORPIO

Kick It Up ACTIVE, PRINCIPLED, STRATEGIC   ***Step It Down*** MANIPULATIVE, FEROCIOUS

November 13

With its generous cutaways, this 1989 Manolo Blahnik lace-up is a deconstructed spin on the classic oxford. How perfectly suited for someone like you, who likes to pick things apart and figure out what makes them tick. Wise, thoughtful, and empathetic, you are a keen observer of life. People-watching is one of your favorite pastimes, as it gives you a deeper understanding of the human psyche. Like this modest, understated shoe, you don't mind receding into the background at times. You prefer to work your magic from behind the scenes, where you can affect people on a deep subconscious level.

Kick It Up OBSERVANT, MODEST, EMPATHETIC　**Step It Down** COVERT, CALCULATING

Opposites attract: a principle you understand well. You are drawn to all things otherwordly and unusual, as there's just so much more to discover in the contrasts. The sinuous black straps of this Donna Karan wedge sandal create a striking juxtaposition to the clear Lucite wedge heel. An intrepid sleuth, you are keen to explore both the dark and the light side of life. Although you don't trust easily, you crave closeness and will search the world to find your soulmate. Like the shoe's snug elastic bands, you will happily twine yourself into a shared life until you're not sure where you begin and the other person ends.

Sign ★ SCORPIO

Kick It Up CURIOUS, INTIMATE, SHARING   ***Step It Down*** CONTROLLING, STANDOFFISH

November 15

Sign ★ SCORPIO

Subliminal cues are not lost on you. With your keen intuition, you respond to the language of music, art, and sensuality. These 1958 Ferragamo evening shoes mirror your elegant sensibilities. The sculptural lace topline dances beguilingly with the shoe's streamlined form and ladylike heel. Its forest-green hue is a nod to your belief in letting things evolve organically, without any force. An expert flirt and a social butterfly, you thrive in the company of beautiful, intriguing people who spark your imagination.

Kick It Up INTUITIVE, ARTSY, FLIRTATIOUS   **Step It Down** VAGUE, SHALLOW

November 16

A **natural detective,** you have an eye for identifying patterns and cracking codes. Systematizing, categorizing, and making the abstract easier for people to understand: these are your specialties. With its strong geometric lines, this Fendi sandal follows an organizing principle similar to your own. A minimalist, you understand the power of the elemental. The graphic red, black, and tan color scheme of these sandals is basic, yet striking: a powerful paradox indeed. The crisp cutaways echo your passion for deconstructing objects and ideas to see what makes them tick. Endlessly curious, life is a giant puzzle that you're out to solve.

Sign ★ SCORPIO

Kick It Up SHARP, SYSTEMATIC, PROBING **Step It Down** OVERSIMPLIFYING, CONTROLLING

November 17

Star powered and mystical, you gleam like a diamond in the night sky, leaving people wondering, "Who's that girl?" Set against a jet-black body, the gold discs and elegant beadwork of this Oscar de la Renta peep-toe glimmers with your intriguing shine. You're a nocturnal creature who comes to life after sundown, when the world is bathed in enigmatic romance. As the kitten heel of this pump suggests, you're a playful creature who isn't averse to a bit of covert mischief. You'll certainly have your fair share of secrets in this lifetime. Save for a diary kept under lock and key, these stories will remain eternally yours (and yours alone) to delight in.

Kick It Up POWERFUL, ROMANTIC, MISCHIEVOUS   **Step It Down** IMPENETRABLE, AMBIGUOUS

Made in 1885, these moccasins are artifacts of the Nez Percé tribe, natives of the Pacific Northwest. Hunters and gatherers, the Nez Percé people historically traveled with the seasons, living harmoniously with nature's cycles. With your heightened sensitivity and awareness, you are tuned in to the rhythm of life. Unspoken cues are not lost on you, and you believe in the power of divine timing. You'll wait patiently for opportunity to present itself, trusting that the right moment will inevitably come. Like the moccasin's gorgeously intricate beading, you are a master of the finer details. It's the little things that mean the most and make the biggest difference in your world.

Kick It Up HARMONIOUS, PATIENT, AWARE   *Step It Down* LANGUID, FIXATED

November 19

Like an incandescent flame, this Stella McCartney colorblock pump shifts from hot pink to red to orange. You're quite the firecracker yourself: passionate, fierce, and hot blooded. Like the clear acrylic heel, you believe in transparency. You're willing to bare your soul in the name of championing a cause. Although you're a feisty one, you lay your cards on the table. People always know where they stand with you, which saves you from the Scorpio pitfall of holding grudges. "You cannot shake hands with a clenched fist," said Indira Gandhi, who shares your birthday. A peaceful warrior, your openhearted energy ultimately turns your adversaries into allies.

Kick It Up FIERY, OUTSPOKEN, LOVABLE   **Step It Down** TACTLESS, CONFRONTATIONAL

November 20

Capable, confident, and commanding, you've got it all zipped up, just like this vintage Balmain heel from the 1980s. The gold fastener wraps seductively around the vamp of the shoe, opening to a tantalizing d'Orsay cutaway. Selectively revealing information is one of your secret weapons. A master strategist, you know exactly what to say and do—and what not to—in order to have the world eating out of the palm of your hand. The juxtaposition of black leather and metal hardware gives this pump a punky edge. There's a rebellious spirit living in you too. When someone lays down the gauntlet, you won't back down without a fight.

Sign ★ SCORPIO

Kick It Up STRATEGIC, COMMANDING, FEARLESS   ***Step It Down*** COMBATIVE, CUNNING

November 21

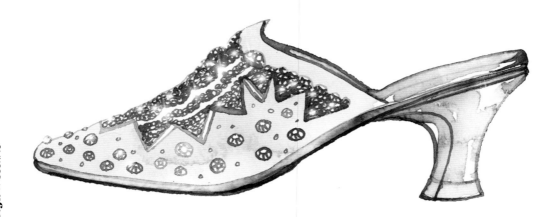

This beaded glass mule was inspired by Cinderella's slipper; a perfect fit for her alone. Fervently individualistic, you favor one-of-a-kind objects and made-to-order luxuries. You're no diva, though. As hardworking as Cinderella herself, you understand the power of paying your dues and may have weathered a few "wicked stepsisters" in your day. In spite of that, you never become bitter. Like the mule's delicate white silk, your optimistic outlook remains unsullied by any hardships you weather. Your loving spirit is pure and radiant, which is why, inevitably, your prince will come.

Kick It Up LUXURIOUS, HARDWORKING, LOVING *Step It Down* NAIVE, MATERIALISTIC

November 22

Sporty, active, and on the go, this Michael Kors sneaker matches the spring in your step. A traveler and adventuress, you like to be in motion at all times. The metallic-gold fabric adds a dash of flash, just as you can sometimes be flamboyant and over the top. It's all in good fun. While you may not stick around till "last call," you're always the one who gets the party started. Patience is not your strong suit, but courage certainly is. You're willing to leap when a new experience catches your fancy. Fortunately, you're a lucky Sagittarius, and you always land on your feet.

Kick It Up ADVENTUROUS, FLAMBOYANT, WILLING   *Step It Down* IMPATIENT, SUPERFICIAL

November 23

This woven wedge sandal comes from Lanvin, Paris's oldest fashion house in operation. The timeless appeal of this exquisitely made shoe echoes your appreciation for things of lasting value. You treasure history, tradition, and anything with a rich storyline attached. You're an entertaining raconteur with a stellar sense of humor, and people love listening as you recount tales and share the trivia that you collect on your travels. The beachy rope strap and jute heel form a striking juxtaposition to the elegant gold leather panels. You have similar range, flowing from casual to formal without missing a beat.

Kick It Up CLASSIC, CULTURED, ENTERTAINING   **Step It Down** ELITIST, BOASTFUL

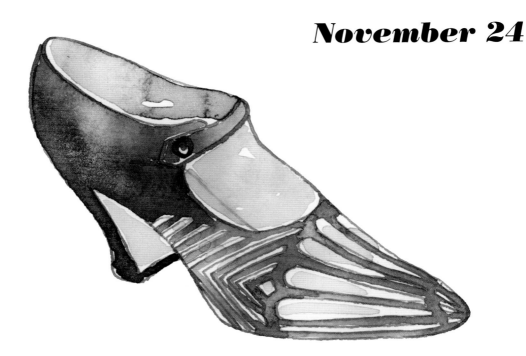

This sprightly 1925 Art Deco pump looks like it was plucked straight from a Moulin Rouge painting by Henri de Toulouse-Lautrec. The artist, who was born today, shared your free-spirited nature. Here to experience *la vie bohème*, you're a social butterfly with an unquenchable thirst for fresh experiences. With its petal-like curves and repeating stack of triangles, this shoe distinguishes itself from the pack. Originality is a trait that you prize. You're not interested in being like everyone else, and you'll go to great lengths to develop your own signature style. Lively and entertaining, you're an incredible hostess, throwing unforgettable fetes that last until the early morning.

Kick It Up BOHEMIAN, ORIGINAL, FUN   ***Step It Down*** OVERINDULGENT, DEFIANT

November 25

Like this patent leather Mary Jane from Doc Martens, you're an adorably tough cookie. Although you can be girlishly sweet at times, you're not to be messed with. You are a woman of ideals who is driven to accomplish something magnificent in this lifetime. With its treaded sole, this resilient buckle shoe was made to go the distance. Similarly, you've got drive and stamina in spades. Like billionaire philanthropist Andrew Carnegie, who shares your birthday, you are here to be a self-made woman. No matter where you begin, you'll work your way up through the ranks until you reach the heights of success.

Kick It Up DRIVEN, TOUGH, SELF-MADE   *Step It Down* FORCEFUL, CONSUMED

November 26

You're quite the exotic creature, as this "Vivian" wedge sandal from Michael Kors suggests. With its stunning giraffe print, this shoe bears distinctive markings, just as you are a true one of a kind yourself. You don't actively try to stand out in the crowd—you simply do. Not that you stay in any particular crowd for too long. Like the ever-migrating giraffe, you are a wanderer, and the shoe's towering wedge mirrors your desire to climb to exciting new heights. For you, life is an endless safari. Your gypsy soul guides you through many "adventures in the wild," winning you a friend in every port.

Kick It Up EXOTIC, WORLDLY, ADVENTUROUS   *Step It Down* FLIGHTY, RUTHLESS

November 27

One-way ticket to Electric Lady-land, please. Like birthday mate Jimi Hendrix, you set the world on fire with your dynamic presence. You're not always "on," though. The element of surprise is your secret weapon. Like the earthy-brown and snakeskin panels of these Jimmy Choo sneakers, you prefer to camouflage yourself while you work tirelessly to master your craft. Then, *bam!* People don't always know what hit them when you unleash your larger-than-life talents. With your serpentine allure, you're part "Voodoo Child," charming people with your mystical dance. You know when to bring it back down to earth too, shedding your secretive skin and letting your sporty, active side out to play.

Kick It Up SURPRISING, DYNAMIC, TALENTED   ***Step It Down*** SECRETIVE, DISTANT

November 28

Like a butterfly bursting from her cocoon, you are the queen of transformation. You thrill at the opportunity to change, improve, or otherwise revolutionize the world around you. The silver straps of this Prada wedge seem to trace the outline of a mariposa's wing. Active and athletic, you're light on your feet, as the cork heel suggests. While you may float like a butterfly, you can also sting like a bee. The bold orange stripe shares your dynamic verve. You don't hold back when you have a point to make, a song to sing, or a talent to put on display.

Sign ★ SAGITTARIUS

Kick It Up TRANSFORMATIVE, ATHLETIC, OUTSPOKEN   ***Step It Down*** SHREWD, TACTLESS

November 29

These boudoir slippers hail from 1865 and were worn in a lady's "evening sitting room." Behind closed doors, the Victorian woman was free to express her truest thoughts without reproach. A revolutionary and philosopher, you live in the world of high concepts and avant-garde ideas. Since you're a few steps ahead of the world, you may do your best work in private, or with a select few. The majestic purple velvet and quilting fabric are the color of royalty, magic, and mystery. The regal Queen of New Ideas, your vision will ultimately shine like the slipper's gemstone buckle. Be patient! You'll have to wait for the world to catch up.

Kick It Up VISIONARY, INTELLIGENT, REGAL   *Step It Down* IMPATIENT, CAGEY

Like this Kate Spade "Gemma" sandal, you evoke classic style and au courant trends in equal measure. You understand the rules of etiquette, but that doesn't mean you'll always play by them. The ladylike bow and delicate straps get a delightful kick from the punchy print of the shoe's fabric. The aquatic blues and greens of the batik blur together like an underwater scene. Similarly, you have a gift for "going with the flow." Although you're a stellar planner, you are willing to turn the tide at a moment's notice if spontaneity unveils a more entertaining idea.

Kick It Up SASSY, SHARP, SPONTANEOUS   **Step It Down** MERCURIAL, VAGUE

November 22 – December 21 **Sagittarius**

DECEMBER

December 22 – January 20 **Capricorn**

December 1

Vibrant and dynamic, you're not afraid to let your true colors show. In fact, you'll wear them proudly like this "Tri Colour Wave" heel from Prada. When life gets too placid, you're the one who creates ripples in the pond, with a wave as lively as the shape of the heel and as whimsical as the suede stripes. You're not a rebel for rebel's sake, though. Deeply philosophical, you believe that people should develop their own well-formed opinions. You have plenty of your own, which you are happy to share with candor, insight, and your signature dose of sidesplitting humor.

Kick It Up CANDID, WITTY, ENERGIZING   ***Step It Down*** DOGMATIC, ARGUMENTATIVE

December 2

With your rainbow-bright disposition, you may read as a happy-go-lucky party girl. Ha! First impressions hardly tell your story. You are a layered and nuanced game-changer who lives to add color and spice to people's lives. Happiness, you believe, is everyone's birthright, and your life's work may involve uplifting the masses. Like this iconic Ferragamo platform, which was designed with the heel raised only slightly above the toe, you're surprisingly well balanced and grounded. Although it irks you when others underestimate your capabilities, you also enjoy the dramatic impact of shock value. When you reveal the fullness of your star-quality personality, jaws may hit the ground, giving you the last (and best) laugh.

Kick It Up ENTHUSIASM, EMPATHY, DRIVE   ***Step It Down*** IMPATIENCE, SELF-DESTRUCTIVENESS

December 3

"Keep it simple" may be your motto, but you always seem to add an unparalleled flourish to all that you do. This sophisticated "Alec" half d'Orsay heel from 3.1 Philip Lim doesn't scream for attention. Upon closer inspection, however, the elegantly defining details—like the asymmetrical cutaways and the curved, unbroken leather— reveal that this is no ordinary shoe. Similarly, you know how to work the element of surprise, doing things so brilliantly unexpected that people stand back in awe. Your attention to your craft can be downright consuming at times. Creating something masterful is your mission in life.

Sign ★ SAGITTARIUS

Kick It Up MASTERFUL, SOPHISTICATED, SURPRISING   *Step It Down* WORK-OBSESSED, UNCOMMUNICATIVE

December 4

Welcome to the jungle! The pandemonium, competition, and wild goings-on may intimidate some, but you're right at home in the action. Like this Jimmy Choo "Fever" sandal, you are not here to be tamed. The chain straps are decorative, but they can't hold you back. You easily slip beyond confines and break free—this is your nature. Driven and fierce, you want to play the game of life without wasting a drop of passion. You can be fearless when it comes to achieving your grand goals in life. Some people find you intimidating, but those who can hang in are in for a thrilling—and glamorous—ride!

Kick It Up WILD, COURAGEOUS, GUNG HO **Step It Down** FEROCIOUS, CUTTHROAT

December 5

Bright, brilliant orange: the color associated with Lady Luck. Like this plucky vintage pump from the seventies, you love to take gambles. And why not? No matter how outrageous the situation, you always seem to land on your feet. Life, for you, is most exhilarating when you are rolling the dice on a new adventure. Good thing you're born on such an auspicious day. As you gain greater wisdom, you become more directed about where and with whom you'll take chances. With your radar honed to a greater degree, you'll inevitably hit the jackpot.

Kick It Up FORTUNATE, CAPRICIOUS, BRAVE   *Step It Down* SHORTSIGHTED, WASTEFUL

December 6

The classic Converse high-top transforms into an indie style sensation thanks to a collaboration with Finnish fashion house Marimekko. A dynamic duo indeed, and totally in synch with your philosophy in life. Pairing up is where it's at for you: you love joining forces with fellow creative types and developing projects and products together. With your gift for spotting up-and-coming talent, you'd also make a fabulous agent. Few things please you more than nurturing another person's artistic streak and cultivating genius in the ones you love. Constantly on the go, you lead a life as bright and fun as the colorblocked pattern of these sneakers.

Kick It Up GIVING, CREATIVE, MOTIVATING ***Step It Down*** DEPENDENT, EXHAUSTED

With its Lucite heels in red, yellow, and green, this "Rainbow Road" wedge could quite literally stop traffic. That's the point, isn't it? You quite like being the center of attention, especially when you are bubbling with an idea for a new creative venture or project. While highly imaginative, you can be honest to the point of transparency, and this makes people feel that they can trust you. This blue peep-toe come from the aptly named design house Poetic Licence, and you take plenty of liberties when it comes to expressing yourself. A true original, you have a range as wide as the color spectrum. You're also a total free spirit, and like the red butterflies adorning the toe, you might just take wing at a moment's notice.

Kick It Up INSPIRED, EXPRESSIVE, FREE   ***Step It Down*** FLIGHTY, BOASTFUL

December 8

You love them; you love them not. Like this Christian Louboutin "Architek" slingback, you tend to be very black and white about things. It's part of being such a passionate soul. When you care about an issue, you'll quickly find a platform, and you can be the most vocal champion for the cause. An eloquent speaker, you attract prominent intellectuals and free thinkers to your inner circle. Be careful, though! You can get heated up quickly. Like the signature crimson splash on the shoe's heel, your firepower can blaze at a temperature that's almost too hot to handle.

Kick It Up PASSIONATE, ELOQUENT, CAUSE-DRIVEN   **Step It Down** TEMPERAMENTAL, IMPATIENT

December 9

Like this intricate Victorian boot, you can be quite a paradox. Your basic makeup is sturdy, but there is also something quite delicate about you, much like the lace panels breaking through the leather. Some may read you as shy, even a tad mysterious. You're certainly not an open book. Unlacing your secrets can be a puzzling task for those bold enough to try. That said, you will espouse your honest opinion—and quite vocally—if asked. More than anything, you prefer to be known for the work that you produce. You're not the flashy type, but you certainly have plenty of sparkle.

Sign ★ SAGITTARIUS

Kick It Up INTRIGUING, MULTIDIMENSIONAL, DEEP   *Step It Down* SECRETIVE, CONFUSING

December 10

Sign ★ SAGITTARIUS

Just as a high priestess perched on her throne, your wisdom flows from a deep and mystical source. You are almost otherworldly in nature, drawing people into your web without even trying. Your magic formula is as hard to replicate as this Peruvian boot, crafted by artisans in the Andes. Bright, colorful, and free spirited, you are a traveler who likes to roam the Earth, collecting the wisdom of the ancients and learning indigenous customs and lore. A reluctant but natural leader, happiness begins when you accept your place as the tribal leader and matriarchal figure of your friends and family.

Kick It Up MYSTICAL, WISE, MODEST   **Step It Down** RESISTANCE TO LEADERSHIP

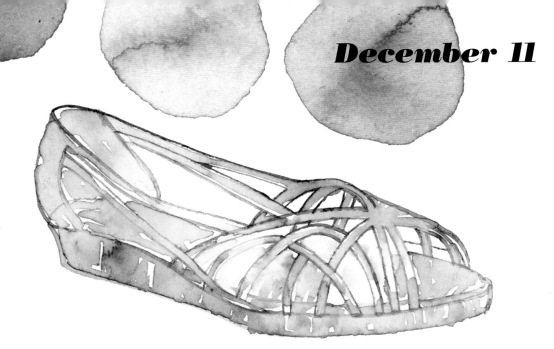

Albert Einstein once said, "The pursuit of truth and beauty is a sphere of activity in which we are permitted to remain children all our lives." With that in mind, it's little wonder you have such an eternally youthful appeal. A visionary and an aesthete, you are forever seeking fresh sources of inspiration. This girlish jelly shoe, a relic of the bright 1980s, is as colorful and as transparent as your personality. Honest to a fault, you simply cannot tell a lie. Although you may put your foot in your mouth at times, your genuinely pure innocence always gets you out of jams.

Kick It Up ETERNALLY YOUTHFUL, COLORFUL, HONEST   *Step It Down* NAIVE, GULLIBLE

December 12

Where will you aim your archer's arrows next? Like the dynamic V accenting this Chanel ankle bootie, you are forever pointing toward a target. There's nothing accidental about your actions. Sure, you're willing to take a gamble here and there, but only for a very specific purpose. You have a keen sense of direction and make an excellent leader and navigator. There's not much room for gray in your black-and-white universe, but that's because you're on a mission. "Time waits for no one" could be your motto. Anyone who wishes to remain in stride with you had better be prepared to pick up the pace!

Kick It Up DIRECTED, SHARP, ACCOMPLISHED   ***Step It Down*** INFLEXIBLE, INTOLERANT

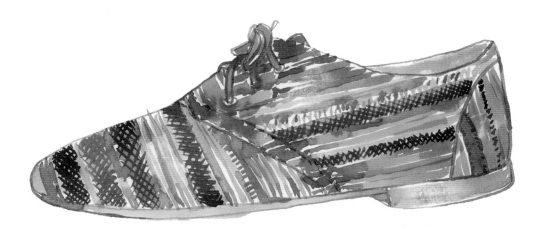

This Osborne classic "Corte" oxford is a sartorialist's dream. Made from hand woven fabric reclaimed from Mayan skirts, it is a work of meticulous craftsmanship. The maker of this repurposed fabric was obviously a lover of stunningly intricate details, much like you. Whatever your path in life, it's essential that you love the process enough to become totally immersed in it. If it takes you hours, months, even years to accomplish your vision, so be it. You'll have something stunning to share with the world when you're through, which might just land you in the history books.

Kick It Up PRECISE, CAPABLE, DETAIL-ORIENTED   **Step It Down** OBSESSED, MISGUIDED

December 14

Considered auspicious symbols in many cultures, dragons are the embodiment of primordial power. With your ability to manipulate the unseen forces of the universe, it's no wonder so many people consider you their lucky totem. Like this crimson Chinese wedding shoe, you can be quite flamboyant and theatrical on the surface. Are you simply being fierce? Or are you sending out smoke signals to distract the competition? You'll never reveal your secret formula for success. People will simply have to watch your display of fireworks and wonder just how you work your magic.

Kick It Up FLAMBOYANT, PRIMAL, ENTERTAINING   *Step It Down* CALCULATING, IRATE

December 15

Is it a sandal, a bootie, a peep-toe, or . . . all of the above? Like this versatile Michael Kors platform, you've got serious range. Any puzzle that's too easy to solve simply bores you. You prefer to unbuckle life's complexities one metal hardware detail at a time. Like the basic black leather and wood heel, you know how to create magic with elemental ingredients. Entrepreneurial and start-up ventures entice you. You're interested in building things from scratch as well as supporting the nascent dreams of loved ones and fellow visionaries.

Kick It Up VERSATILE, CLEVER, ENTREPRENEURIAL   ***Step It Down*** SCATTERED, NOSY

December 16

A **romantic idealist,** you are happiest when you're in the flush of new amore. You love to learn the curves and arcs of a stranger's personality. If intrigued, you can quickly adapt to his rhythm, falling in perfect step with your new paramour. This Argentine tango shoe helps you glide through your favorite moves without missing a beat. Here's a truth you understand innately: what looks easy on the surface is often the most complex lesson to grasp. Good thing you so love a challenge. Anything too simplistic will not hold your interest for long. Some might call you obsessive, but you're just dedicated to mastering your craft.

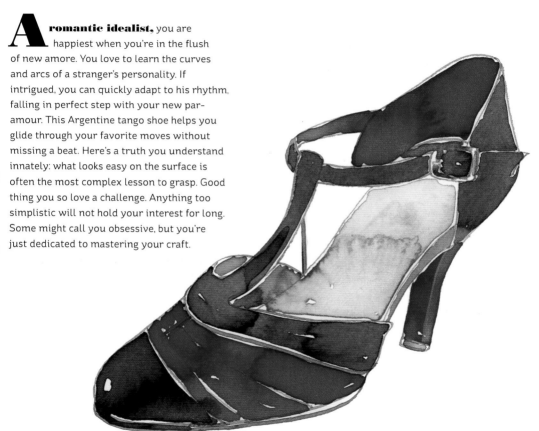

Kick It Up ADAPTABLE, CHARISMATIC, MASTERFUL   **Step It Down** GULLIBLE, MISGUIDED

December 17

Like this Michael Kors fringed flat boot you have a solidly down-to-earth charm. A reliable soul with a hard-core work ethic, you believe in the importance of walking your talk. Because of your high level of personal integrity, people trust you with weightier matters, and you will hold many secrets for people throughout your life. You always dish out stellar advice, knowing how to combine practical wisdom with gleaming optimism, the perfect combination to help people get back on their feet. You have a wild streak too, although it tends to be hidden beneath a serious outer layer. Being rowdy upon occasion is good for your soul, so seek out friends and lovers who can set you free from that self-imposed corral.

Sign ★ SAGITTARIUS

Kick It Up RELIABLE, EMPOWERING, HARDWORKING   ***Step It Down*** STERN, REPRESSED

December 18

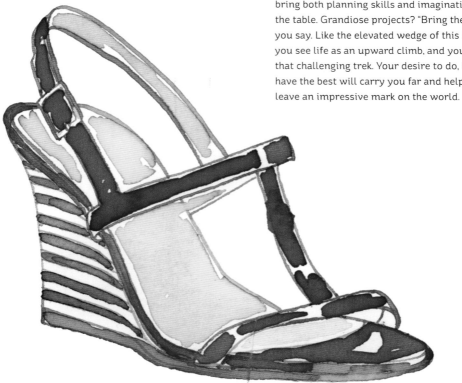

Like the graphically striped heel of this Kate Spade "Lorna" T-strap wedge, you love it when the details all line up in perfect order. You are an organizer and architect of life, and people count on you to bring both planning skills and imagination to the table. Grandiose projects? "Bring them on!" you say. Like the elevated wedge of this sandal, you see life as an upward climb, and you crave that challenging trek. Your desire to do, be, and have the best will carry you far and help you leave an impressive mark on the world.

Kick It Up ACCOMPLISHED, ORGANIZED, CHIC   **Step It Down** CRITICAL, UPTIGHT

December 19

They definitely broke the mold when they made you. Complex and daring, you're neither built nor wired like most people. Originality is your calling card, and your interests are as varied as your moods. A bit of an attention seeker, you actually enjoy it when people stop and stare at you. With your many layers, you can be a bit puzzling to dissect, but like the architectural detailing of this Balenciaga loafer, the pieces all come together brilliantly. Your life is meant to be a fascinating collage of worldly experiences, encounters, and escapades.

Sign ★ SAGITTARIUS

Kick It Up ORIGINAL, INTRIGUING, DIVERSE ***Step It Down*** PUZZLING, OSTENTATIOUS

December 20

The lady pioneer who wore this 1890s-era boot was surely dedicated to breaking new ground. While you may not be riding in a covered wagon, you are an undeniable trailblazer. Your favorite place is at the front of the line. This is not necessarily because you are competitive—although you do have a spirited drive—but rather because you so richly enjoy the act of discovery. Curious to the core, when your internal compass points toward a gold rush, wild horses couldn't drag you away from your mission. Your unflagging enthusiasm is infectious, which is why you always have a caravan of followers close on your heels.

Kick It Up TRAILBLAZING, INNOVATIVE, EXCITING ***Step It Down*** IMPULSIVE, GULLIBLE

December 21

With its punk-inspired hardware, there's more than a hint of naughtiness to this Valentino "Rockstud" pump. The peep-toe is surreptitiously suggestive, revealing a hint without giving everything away. Similarly, you are seductive to the point of being disarming, a master of strategy who knows just how to get her way. This stiletto heel is sky-high, just like your ambitions, but when it comes to achieving your ends, you're not one to go for the direct hit. You prefer to play coy, which always leaves the world eating right out of your pretty little hand. As a born thrillseeker, playing with fire is an irresistible temptation. Thanks to your quick and clever mind, you rarely get burned.

Sign ★ SAGITTARIUS

Kick It Up RADICAL, AMBITIOUS, ALLURING   ***Step It Down*** IMPULSIVE, HEDONISTIC

December 22

Active and on the move, you walk with a go-getter's spring in your step. You're here to accomplish something major, which means you can't afford to waste a moment standing still. These Christian Louboutin "Rantus Orlato" sneakers will keep you light on your feet as you steadily work toward your goals. Their gold detail is as bright as the lightbulbs that pop off in your imagination every five seconds. Patience is not your strong suit. When you have an idea, your next instinct is to race ahead and make it happen!

Kick It Up MOTIVATED, PEPPY, POSITIVE   *Step It Down* IMPETUOUS, EXHAUSTING

December 23

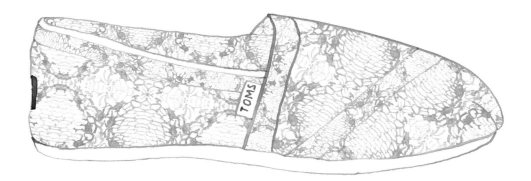

Kind, reliable, and hardworking, you're a salt-of-the-earth kind of gal. Variety is not the spice of your life. Rather, your heart is warmed by traditions, which are the thread that bind you to your community. A natural leader as well as a nurturer, you inevitably play the role of the matriarch among friends and family. This knitting wool TOMS shoe speaks to your comforting, down-to-earth personality. Known for their philanthropic mission and timeless appeal, they are exceptionally warm, just like you. The woven pattern reflects your "back to basics" maxim. Nothing too fancy is required to make you happy—just swaddle you in love, and you're all smiles.

Kick It Up RELIABLE, DOWN-TO-EARTH, NURTURING   ***Step It Down*** OLD-FASHIONED, MYOPIC

December 24

Love may be a battlefield, but you're willing to walk through the fire when your heart says yes. With its complex curves and solid heel, this Miu Miu peep-toe velvet bow pump is both dreamy and stable—a paradox that you pull off with aplomb. A hard-core romantic, no one would accuse you of being hopeless: you're far too together for that. It's just that your devotion to the ones you adore could take you to the ends of the Earth. Partnership oriented, you match up easily with a variety of folks, just like the black of these shoes; which, incidentally, is anything but basic.

Kick It Up DEVOTED, LOVING, STABLE   *Step It Down* COMPLICATED, SOMBER

December 25

With your boundless generosity, you may have already earned your place in heaven. Vivienne Westwood's "Wing" sandal was a tribute to the Greek God Hermes, who was known for being a great messenger. Similarly, you are here to light the way for people, helping them connect to higher truths and wisdom. Made from nontoxic, recyclable plastic, these sandals are the vanguard of ecofriendly couture fashion. Perfect, since as an earth sign, you are concerned with preserving and conserving. Good thing you don't have to sacrifice your offbeat style in the process.

Kick It Up ANGELIC, OFFBEAT, CHARITABLE   *Step It Down* UNGROUNDED, SACRIFICIAL

December 26

"**Nothing is more simple** than greatness; indeed, to be simple is to be great," said Transcendentalist essayist Ralph Waldo Emerson. Your own ascension does not lie in a complex formula, but rather in your willingness to practice your passions to the point of perfection. This "Lisbon" work boot from Seychelles mirrors your unassuming ethos. Elegant without being flashy, earthy without being plain, you believe in earning your stripes based on merit rather than manipulating the forces of the universe. Your well-deserved place at the top of the heap awaits. Keep on climbing!

Kick It Up MODEST, ELEGANT, THOROUGH   *Step It Down* MEEK, OVERWORKED

December 27

The **intricate laces** of this gothic boot are as tempting as they are forbidding. This seductive paradox is one you understand well. Your "come hither" stare is sexy and alluring, but you want people advancing only so close. Deeply private, you need a good amount of personal space to keep your soul in balance. You have a fascination with life's mysteries and don't mind exploring the darker side of matters. At times you can be prone to pessimism, but your ability to figure out the potential risks and pitfalls also saves you from costly missteps.

Sign ★ CAPRICORN

Kick It Up SEDUCTIVE, MYSTICAL, AWARE   *Step It Down* PESSIMISTIC, FORBIDDING

December 28

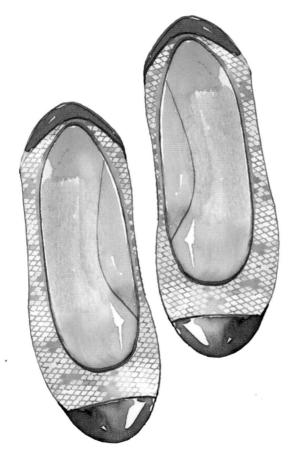

You bring a glimmer of glamour to all that you do, like these sparkly "Delia" ballet flats from Coach. Playful and fun loving, you have a bit of a mischievous streak. You never get too far out of step with the rules, however, as you're more interested in bending them than in breaking them. When you feel inspired by a mission, you can be a vocal, capable leader—and you don't mind breaking a sweat in the name of reaching your lofty goals. Throughout it all, you manage to keep your feet planted on solid ground, and your practical nature is as strong as your fanciful streak.

Kick It Up CAPABLE, GLAMOROUS, PRAGMATIC   **Step It Down** TENTATIVE, HARD-NOSED

December 29

Decadent yet sophisticated, this jewel-toned Manolo will never go out of style. Similarly, you're the picture of timeless, classic grace. With little to no effort, you attract elite people into your sphere. The truth: you're a bit of a society lady at heart. As you move through life, your contact database may become your grandest treasure trove. You need no excuses to dress to the nines. Every day is a special occasion as far as you're concerned, and like the buckle on this Blahnik, you really know how to work the sparkle.

Kick It Up SOPHISTICATED, POPULAR, ATTRACTIVE   *Step It Down* SNOBBISH, SPOILED

December 30

Sign ★ CAPRICORN

An enchanted engineer, you not only dream up fantastical ideas, but you also figure out how to build them into a soundly structured reality. Like the leaves on this strappy Donna Karan sandal, you have a sylphlike sweetness about you. Your imagination is your charm, your leadership skills your calling card. You're also quite resourceful. Like this sandal's wood and raffia heel, you prefer to work with natural elements, harvesting the best from what already exists rather than manufacturing it from something artificial. Spotting the genius in other people is one of your gifts, and you love to develop talented souls into shining stars.

Kick It Up CREATIVE, ANALYTICAL, THOROUGH   **Step It Down** EXACTING, IMPATIENT

December 31

With your indomitable spirit, you're the walking definition of a steel magnolia. The machinery you're made of is built to last, much like the industrial embellishments on this Alexander McQueen "Titanic" bootie. A bit intimidating, you naturally assume a position of authority in all that you do. You don't mean to be bossy, but sometimes you just can't help but take charge. The gears of your mind are razor-sharp, and you enjoy figuring out the way things work. That way, you can later break them apart and rebuild them with your own patented flair.

Kick It Up RESILIENT, AUTHORITATIVE, SHARP   *Step It Down* INTIMIDATING, DOMINATING

About the Authors

Identical twin sisters **Tali and Ophira Edut**—known as the AstroTwins—are professional astrologers with twenty years of experience in astrology, publishing, and coaching. With a mission to "bring the stars down to Earth," they combine mystical knowledge with real-world advice.

The AstroTwins are the official astrologers for Elle.com and myLifetime.com, and the authors of *The AstroTwins' Love Zodiac*. Through their columns and their website AstroStyle.com, their predictions reach millions each month. Tali and Ophira have read charts for celebrities, including Beyoncé, Stevie Wonder, and Sting. Their astrological insight has been featured by MTV, the *New York Times*, the Style Network, E!, and Sirius/XM radio.

With their unique applied method of astrology and coaching, the AstroTwins help clients and readers "de-sign" amazing lives. They are available for private consultation, by appointment, through AstroStyle.com.

About the Illustrator

Samantha Hahn is a Manhattan-based illustrator and blogger known for her watercolors with sartorial flair. She earned her BFA from Syracuse University and an MA from Columbia University.

Samantha illustrates for a range of editorial, publishing, advertising, branding, and licensing clients who include: Random House, Assouline, Chronicle, Storey, *Condé Nast Traveler*, *Glamour*, *Marie Claire*, *Surface* magazine, Anthropologie, Tiffany & Co., Daily Candy, Galison, teNeues, and Saatchi & Saatchi.

Her work has been featured in numerous art and design books in addition to the books she illustrates.

Her blog, Maquette, features art, design, and style for the visually hungry. You can also find Samantha on Pinterest.

samanthahahn.com
samanthahahn.com/blog